A DICTIONARY
FOR YACHTSMEN

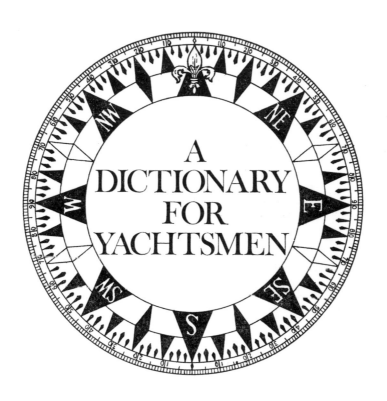

A
DICTIONARY
FOR
YACHTSMEN

FRANCIS H. BURGESS

DAVID & CHARLES

NEWTON ABBOT LONDON

NORTH POMFRET (VT) VANCOUVER

0 7153 6344 1

Library of Congress Catalog Card Number 74–81218

© Francis H. Burgess 1974

Set in 10pt Monotype Baskerville and printed in
Great Britain by Latimer Trend & Company Ltd Plymouth
for David & Charles (Holdings) Limited
South Devon House Newton Abbot Devon

Published in the United States of America
by David & Charles Inc
North Pomfret Vermont 05053 USA

Published in Canada by Douglas David &
Charles Limited 3645 McKechnie Drive
West Vancouver BC

FOREWORD

The language of the sea, always part of our mother tongue, has been handed down to us all, as the heritage of a seafaring nation. Those who spend their life at sea, or live by its shores, and obtain their living or find pleasure from it, use this language as part of their natural life; not only do they speak it, but they come to live and think by it in all they do, for it is a vocabulary made by seamen for seamen. In addition to all those who enjoy yachting, dinghy sailing, or already have the sea 'in their blood', the rising generation of youth and countless others who are now realising the tremendous enjoyment and exhilaration to be found in sailing, boating, or 'messing about in boats' in whatever capacity, will soon discover that it is necessary to know more about these things.

The object of this book, therefore, is to provide a handy reference glossary of nautical terms, arranged as a dictionary of short but concise explanations whereby practically any meaning may be easily and quickly found.

It will be apparent that the preservation of our nautical language is not only important, but essential, for inasmuch as all seamen are frequently judged by their use and knowledge of it, it follows that one cannot hope to be a good seaman, or to own, use, or sail a yacht or boat unless one acquires a good working knowledge, which implies knowing and calling things and actions by their proper names, so as to be understood, and to understand others.

F.H.B.

A1 The symbol used to classify a vessel's construction and equipment, etc, when first class in *Lloyd's Register of Shipping.*

Aback A sail with its clew to windward or pressed back against the mast with the wind on the fore side of it, tending to give the vessel sternway or drive her to leeward. Sails are 'laid aback' purposely to deaden the way, and are 'taken aback' when brought about by bad steering or change of wind; 'all aback forward' is the warning cry from forward to the helmsman; and 'taken aback' means suddenly surprised or flabbergasted.

Abaft Behind. At or near the stern. Aft of amidships. On the after side of.

Abaft the beam Bearing more than 90° from dead ahead.

Abandonment The surrender of all claims to ownership of an insured vessel to the underwriters.

Abate The wind is said to abate when its force lessens.

Abeam At right-angles to the fore-and-aft line. In line with the beams.

Able seaman An experienced seaman, able to hand, reef, and steer, and competent to carry out all duties on deck or in boats.

Aboard, inboard On, or in, any vessel or boat. On board.

About A vessel is said to be about when she has filled on her new tack.

About ship An order given to prepare to go about. To tack.

Abox Term applied to yards of a mast that are braced in the opposite direction to those on a neighbouring mast; a handy way to keep a vessel under control.

Abreast Side by side in a direction at right-angles with the keel. In line abeam on a parallel course with bows all in line.

Accidental gybe Should the wind get on the same quarter as the mainsail is set, when running, and get behind the sail, it may slam the latter across unexpectedly with extreme violence—one of the most dangerous possibilities while sailing.

Acockbill With ends pointing upwards: applied to an anchor hanging from the hawse pipe; also to yards topped up by one lift for use as a derrick, or as a sign of mourning.

Across the tide A vessel at anchor sets across the tide when the wind is stronger than the tide and blowing in the opposite direction.

Adjustments of compasses The placing of magnets and iron in close

7

proximity to a compass to compensate for the error caused by the magnetism in the ship.

Admiralty hitch The marlinespike hitch (see p 113).

Admiralty pattern anchor An anchor so made that its stock can be folded down; its arms and shank are fixed, while the stock is fitted up at right-angles to the arms.

Admiralty sweep An extra large turning circle made to approach a gangway or come alongside a vessel in a boat.

Adrift Floating on the tide unsecured, or applied to anything that has become unfastened, been carried away, broken loose, or been mislaid.

Advance That amount of movement of a vessel, on her course, after helm has been applied.

Adze The shipbuilder's axe; an essential boatbuilding tool, for dubbing flat and circular work.

Affreightment The hiring or chartering of any vessel.

Afloat Floating. On the water. At sea.

Afore Before. Forward of.

Aft Towards, at, or near the stern.

After end That part of a vessel abaft the beam, nearest the stern.

After jiggermast The after mast in a six-masted vessel.

After mizzenmast The fourth mast in a five- or six-masted vessel.

After part That part of a vessel near the stern.

After peak The small store or space forward of the stern frame, usually enclosed on its fore side by a collision bulkhead (see p 44).

After swim The underwater curvature of the hull, permitting the sweep-in of water to act on the screws and rudder.

Aftermost An object identified as that nearest the stern.

Afternoon The afternoon watch, from noon to 4 pm, but often worked from 12.30 to fit in with lunch.

Aground The state of a vessel part of which is touching bottom. Not completely waterborne. Held fast on the bottom.

Ahead Before. Forward of. Advance. In the direction of the bows.

Ahoy The general nautical hailing term to attract attention.

Ahull Hove to, and driven before

the wind broadside on or stern first, with all canvas furled.

Alee   To leeward. Down wind. Away from the wind. On the lee side.

All aback   With all sails aback. Startled (see **Aback**).

All aboard   A collective order to embark. Embarkation completed.

All a-taunto   With everything set up, squared up, and shipshape.

All fast   Denotes that a rope is belayed or secured.

All fours   Describes a vessel when laid up, or moored, with warps from each bow and quarter.

All hands   All the crew. The call to muster every available hand on-board, mostly used when the watch below is required to assist the watch on deck.

All in the wind   So close to the wind that all sails begin to shake.

All standing   With everything provided being set up, and in use.

Aloft   Above the upper deck, usually meaning high up. At the masthead.

Aloft there   The correct hail to anyone aloft.

Alongside   By the side of a ship. Waiting at a gangway or steps. Lengthwise in line with, and made fast to, any jetty, pier, etc. Two vessels berthed side by side together are 'lying alongside' each other.

Alow   Below. Near the deck or below it. Low down. Not aloft.

Alow and aloft   Below decks and above. From top to bottom. High and low.

Alternating light   A navigational distinguishing light that shows alternately in different colours.

American whipping   Similar to a common whipping except that both ends are brought up at the centre and reef-knotted.

Amidships   The middle part of a ship, either in a fore-and-aft line or athwartships. A helm order to put the wheel or tiller in position so that the rudder is fore and aft.

Amphibian   A loose term covering all vehicles and craft so fitted that they may be propelled on both land and water.

Anchor   A heavy metal implement used to retain a vessel by temporarily chaining it to the sea bed at any selected point. There are many different patterns and sizes for various purposes. Each large ship's equipment is covered by statute.

Anchor bed A strongly made fitting on each side of the forecastle, used for stowing and securing stocked anchors.

Anchor bell The bell, placed forward, when at anchor during fog, and rung as prescribed in the Rule of the Road; sometimes used to denote the number of shackles out when working cable.

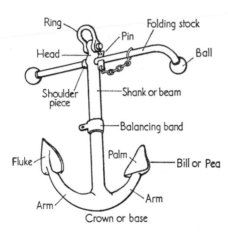

Parts of an anchor

Anchor buoy A small marking buoy with its mooring rope (called the buoyrope) attached to the crown of an anchor to indicate its position.

Anchor chain The chain used to anchor a ship, usually called the cable.

Anchor light The all-round white light, sometimes known as the riding light, carried by all vessels at anchor in accordance with the Rule of the Road, and usually hoisted on the fore stay. Ships over 150ft in length carry an additional similar light aft, positioned 15ft lower than the foremost one.

Anchor shackle, anchor link The special shackle used to secure the cable to the anchor.

Anchor, to To cast or lower an anchor to fix a ship in position.

Anchor warp The rope used in small boats when anchoring; it is sometimes reeled, and often referred to as the 'grapnel'.

Anchor watch The continuous vigilance maintained when a vessel is at anchor in rough weather. Special hands are detailed to remain on deck and take bearings, note if the ship drags, and stand by to veer cable or use the other anchor if required.

Anchorage The place where a ship, or ships, may anchor.

Anchor's aweigh The report from the forecastle that the anchor has been hove out of the ground (is off bottom) with its weight taken by the cable.

Anemometer An instrument for measuring the velocity of winds.

Angel's footstool A fancy name given to one of the skysails.

Angle of heel The amount a ship heels when she has a list.

Angulated sails Triangular sails with a girth-band perpendicular to the luff, above which the upper cloths are parallel to the leech, and the lower ones parallel to the foot.

Annual variation The inconsistency in the earth's lines of force that causes a change of variation in the magnetic compass; the difference is printed on charts as increasing or decreasing so much annually.

Answer A vessel is said to answer her helm when she changes direction and obeys the movements of wheel and rudder.

Answering pennant The pennant used to acknowledge a signal. It is hoisted 'at the dip' when the signal is first seen, and then 'close up' when understood (see **Code pendant**, p 44).

Anticyclone An area of high barometric pressure, usually associated with fine weather.

Apeak When the cable is hove short, or 'up and down', and the bows are over the anchor to be broken out, the anchor is said to be apeak.

Apparent wind The difference between the true wind and its direction as changed by the set of the sails or the motion of the observer. For example, if a boat is making 6 knots running before a wind that is blowing at 10 knots, the apparent wind is 4 knots.

Apron The straight-grained timber strengthening the stem and fitted on the after side of it to receive the ends of the planks. The leadsman's canvas safety screen or belt, set up at the 'chains' (see p 37). The surface of a concrete slipway.

Archboard The formed timber which, with the transom, forms the after end of a counter stern.

Arching The old term for 'hogging' (see p 89).

Ardency A quality giving a ship the tendency to head into the wind.

Arisings All the old, damaged, and replaced materials that accumulate when refits or repairs are carried out.

Arming the lead Filling the cavity at the base of the lead with tallow, putty, grease, or soap, etc, to ascertain the nature of the bottom.

Arms The extremities of a yard or boom. The arms of an anchor are that part extending from the crown to each fluke.

Arse The lower end of a block.

Artificial eye Made in the end of a rope by unlaying one strand, shaping the eye required, relaying the strand again in the opposite direction, and tucking the ends to finish off.

Artificial respiration Methods of restoring breathing to an apparently drowned person, and essential knowledge to all seafarers, especially those who use small boats.

Ashore On the land, having left a ship. Aground.

Asleep A sail filled with wind just sufficient to belly it out, but not flapping, is said to be asleep.

Aspect ratio The relation of the length of a sail along its luff to that of its foot; a tall narrow sail has a high aspect ratio, and vice versa.

Astay The position of the cable leading to an anchor, when it is in line with the fore stay, or is 'growing' at a somewhat similar angle.

Astern Behind. Backwards. In the direction of the stern. Outside and abaft a vessel. To 'drop astern' is to go back, or be left behind. To 'go astern' is to make way stern first.

Aswim Afloat.

At anchor A vessel riding by one anchor.

At the dip The position to which the answering pennant is hoisted (6ft below the 'close up' position) to indicate that a signal has been observed but not yet understood or decoded.

Athwart, athwartships In a transverse direction. In the direction of the beams, from side to side. Acrossways.

Athwart the hawse Across the bows.

Athwart the tide Said of a vessel lying across the current.

Atrip An anchor is atrip when it has been broken out of the ground. A sail is atrip when hoisted, sheeted home, ready for trimming.

Automatic helmsman The gyro-controlled machine that works a steering engine so as to keep a vessel on any preselected course.

Auxiliary A yacht primarily used for sailing, but also fitted with motor power for use if necessary.

Avast, 'Vast Stop. Cease. Hold fast.

Awash Applied to whatever the sea, or water, is just washing over. Level with the surface of the water or just under it.

Away aloft The order commanding anyone to climb a mast or rigging.

Aweather To windward.

Aweigh Off the ground.

Awning A canvas protection spread above a deck or over a boat as a shelter from sun or rain.

Awning curtains Canvas screens stopped or laced to hang vertically from the sides of an awning, their lower edges also being stopped down to form a protection against bad weather.

Awning ropes The ridgerope(s) and sideropes supporting an awning.

Aye, aye, sir The recognised verbal acceptance of an order.

Azimuth The distance of a star in angular degrees from the north or south point of a meridian.

Azimuth circle An instrument, containing a mirror and prism, fitted on to a compass to facilitate reading off the bearing of an observed object.

Azimuth compass A compass employed to find the bearing of the sun or other heavenly body. It is similar to an ordinary compass except that the card also has two circles divided into degrees, while the bowl is fitted with sighting frame and mirror.

Baby jib A small jib topsail set high on the outer stay.

Back The keel and keelson of a ship.

Back her An order to put the vessel astern.

Back out Move out stern first. Get out of any difficulty.

Back sailing Hauling the boom of a mainsail or mizzen to windward when a ship loses her way in going about. This forces her head on a new tack, and is a kind of box hauling.

Back ship Work a ship astern by sails or power.

Back splice Used to prevent the ends of a rope from unlaying. A crown knot is formed, and the ends tucked back.

Back, to A wind is said to back when it changes direction anticlockwise. To sheet a sail to windward. To brace a yard against the wind so as to press the canvas to the mast.

Back up Reinforce with extra hands, when a rope is held under strain.

Back water, Back your oars A command used in pulling boats for the oars to be pushed and not pulled, in order to make sternway.

13

Backboard A large portable board fitted athwartships before the transom in small boats as a backrest; it is usually decorative with a name.

Backbone The fore-and-aft centre ridgerope supporting an awning.

Backing and filling A method of alternately filling and then backing sails, to keep a ship in position for a while or when manoeuvring in a narrow channel.

Backrope A small chain or pennant to stay a dolphin striker.

Backset A counter current or eddy.

Backspring A rope led from midships of a vessel to a bollard well aft on the jetty, to prevent her from ranging ahead.

Backstays Wire stays fitted as standing rigging to support a mast against forces acting in an oblique direction. They are led from a mast to a point just abaft it at the ship's side. Additional stays are often set up, and these are called 'preventers' or 'preventer backstays'. In sailing vessels where stays have to be frequently set up or slacked off they are called 'running backstays', and, if transferable, 'shifting backstays'.

Backstrapped Applied to a boat that is carried by wind or tide into any awkward position, and held there. Unable to stem a tide.

Backwinding A foresail set with sheets holding its leech too far inboard will spill its wind into the back of the mainsail by the mast, thus 'backwinding the mainsail'.

Bag reef The short reef of a sail taken to prevent it from bagging on a wind.

Baggywrinkle Fat bunches of yarns, sennet, or other padding made specially to be placed to prevent chafing.

Bagpipe the mizzen Haul the mizzen sheet until the boom is close to the weather shroud and the sail is aback.

Bailer Any small bucket, tin, or pan, or any other receptacle, with which to bail (remove) water from a boat. The person using it.

Balance lug A small-boat term for a lugsail with its foot laced to a boom. When hoisted, it sets with both boom and yard projecting forward of the mast, to which neither is secured.

Balance reef A diagonal reef put in a spanker that makes it into a triangular-shaped sail.

Balanced rudder One in which the stock is not the leading edge but placed abaft it to form two parts. The pressure on the forward area underwater tends to balance that on the after part, thus making it easier to turn.

Balancing band A band on the shank of an anchor, so placed that if lifted at that point the anchor will be raised horizontally.

Bald-headed rig A schooner with gaff-headed sails but no topsails.

Ballast Water, solid matter, or other weight, carried low down in a vessel for purposes of stability.

Ballast logs Timbers lashed alongside a sailing boat to help prevent her from capsizing.

Ballast tanks Compartments holding water, oil, or other liquid that can be pumped from one tank to another for purposes of trim (see p 167).

Balloon sails Extra large sails of light material used as large jibs or spinnakers in yacht racing.

Banderole, bandrol The small swallow-tail or pennant specially used at a masthead as a weather vane.

Bank An area of the sea bed raised above the surrounding ground.

Bank the oars Position men on the thwarts ready for pulling.

Bar The silting-up of deposit or shallowing formed near the entrance to a harbour or inlet. A boom placed across a harbour entrance.

Bar keel A solid metal keel, riveted to the garboards, which projects down outside the plating.

Bar taut Said of any rope stretched rigid under great tension.

Barber hauler A small light block used to control a jib sheet.

Bare pole charter The charter of a vessel only, with no crew.

Bare poles A sailing vessel with no sails set is 'under bare poles'.

Barge A flat-bottomed vessel of shallow draught, with a broad beam and large stowing space; it may be self-propelled or made to be towed. A long narrow flat craft built for canal work. Any special boat built or adapted for ceremonial work.

Barnacles The small shellfish which adhere to a ship's bottom, piers, etc. They do no harm but tend to reduce speed.

Barograph An instrument which automatically charts barometric readings.

Barometer An instrument which measures the pressure of the atmosphere and indicates changes of weather.

Barque A three-, four-, or five-masted sailing vessel, square-rigged but with fore-and-aft sails on the aftermost mast.

Barquentine A three-, four-, or five-masted sailing vessel having square sails on the foremast only.

Barratry Any wrongful act committed by a master or the crew that is to the detriment of the owner or cargo.

Barrel The circular part of a capstan to which hawsers are brought.

Barricoe A small fresh-water cask, as stowed in ship's boats.

Basin An enclosure to accommodate vessels awaiting repair or docking; it may be either tidal or completely enclosed.

Bass Grass line (see p 80).

Bathymetry The art of sounding and measuring depths of the sea. A bathymetric chart shows a contour of the bottom by depth lines.

Batten cleats Brackets fitted to coamings to receive the battens.

Batten down Secure hatchway covers and tarpaulins by means of steel battens wedged on to the coamings.

Batten pockets Long narrow pockets fitted to a yacht's mainsails,

and sometimes jibs, to receive battens to keep the sail taut.

Battens Long light narrow strips of wood. Long narrow metal slats.

Battledore A flat metal bar inserted through the cable bitts and forming a projecting arm each side, to keep the turns from riding.

Bay Any space in the side of a compartment whose width is greater than its depth. An area of the sea extending into a coastline so that the seaward width exceeds the depth of penetration.

Beach The shore. A coastal formation of shingle or sand above the high-water mark.

Beach, to To haul or drive a boat up on the shore. To land anyone.

Beachcomber A long curling wave rolling in from the sea.

Beached Any vessel that has run ashore or is placed there for any reason has been beached.

Beacon A distinctive artificial warning mark to aid navigation.

Beam The breadth of a vessel at her widest part. Extreme breadth. A transverse timber or steel bar to withstand the stresses at the ship's side, and used to support a deck. The stock of an anchor.

Beam ends A vessel is said to be on her beam ends when hove down so that she heels excessively, with her beams at an angle that is more vertical than horizontal. Sometimes used when sailing with the lee rail well awash.

Beam, on the At right angles to the fore-and-aft line of a ship.

Beam reach Sailing with the wind on the beam.

Beam sea A sea rolling in at right-angles to a vessel's course.

Beam wind A wind blowing at right-angles to the keel.

Beamy Anything of unusual or excessive beam; the term 'six-beam vessel', for instance, is sometimes used to denote that her length is six times that of her beam. Other numbers may be substituted for 'six'.

Bear The direction of an object (see **Bearing**).

Bear a hand Assist anyone; usually an injunction to 'hurry and help'.

Bear away Put the tiller up and keep farther away from the wind.

Bear down on Approach anything from windward.

Bear off Push off a boat alongside, for example. Hold off any approaching object. Move away.

Bear up Bear away (see above).

Bearding The rounded fore edge of a rudder and its sternpost recess.

Bearding line A constructional term denoting the line showing the ends of planks or plating at the stem and sternpost.

Bearers The short transverse beams above the keelson in small boats to support the floorboards. The strong timbers fitted fore and aft in boats for the engine bed.

Bearing The direction of one object from another; it may be given as true, magnetic, or relative to the vessel's course.

Bearing finder The azimuth circle (see p 13).

Beat To beat to windward is to keep close hauled on a wind.

Beaufort wind scale A table used at sea to classify the various wind forces and their speeds, their names and descriptions being denoted by the use of numerals.

Force number	Wind speed (knots)	Definition
0	Less than 1	Calm
1	1–3	Light airs
2	4–6	Light breeze

Force number	Wind speed (knots)	Definition
3	7–10	Gentle breeze
4	11–16	Moderate breeze
5	17–21	Fresh breeze
6	22–27	Strong breeze
7	28–33	Moderate gale
8	34–40	Fresh gale
9	41–47	Strong gale
10	48–55	Violent whole gale
11	56–63	Storm
12	64–71	Hurricane

13 to 17 are used for even worse conditions

Becalmed Unable to make way from absence of wind. In the lee of any high obstruction, or of another vessel passing to windward and taking all one's wind. Motionless.

Becket A loop; a small eye fitted to the end of a rope, that it may be tailed to reeve through a block.

Becket bend Sheet bend (see p 146).

Becket of a block The eye in an extension of the cheek straps to take the standing part of a tackle.

Becket rowlock A small rope strop used on a thole pin to contain an oar when rowing.

Becueing The 'scowing' of an anchor, when used on rocky ground.

Bee blocks Pieces of wood with holes through which a rope is rove.

Bees Small wooden strips affixed to a spar as chocks.

Before On the forward side of.

Before the beam Said of any object observed to be less than 90° from right ahead, on either side.

Before the wind Sailing with the wind aft; 'running'.

Belay Make fast a rope round a belaying pin or cleat. A directive to cease what one is doing, or to cancel an order.

Belaying pin A metal pin that fits into a rack on the fiferail or pinrail, and to which a rope may be belayed.

Bell Seagoing vessels must carry a bell at least 12in in diameter, for use in fog; this bell, or an additional one, is also used to denote ship's time, being struck every half-hour. Each 4 hour watch starts and ends at eight bells, one bell being struck for each half-hour. Time on board ship is referred to in 'bells', and not read as from a clock; thus, at 2, 6, and 10 o'clock on shore, the time at sea is 'four bells'.

Bell buoy A buoy containing a bell that is rung by the motion of the sea.

Bell rope The rope on the bell clanger, by which it is rung. It is usually tiddly and ornamental, embodying fancy knots, etc.

18

Belly A sail is said to belly when filled by the wind, or if it is shaped for this purpose. The swell of a sail or awning.

Belly band An extra cloth of canvas fitted to a sail to strengthen it for the reef points.

Belly stay An extra support applied to a mast or spar at its centre.

Belly tackle A tackle used to hold sheer legs together when heavy weights are lifted, and fitted halfway up the spars.

Below Between decks. 'Going below' is descending from the upper deck.

Belting A heavy timber rubbing-strake fitted outside large vessels at or near the waterline.

Benches Any fore-and-aft seats in a boat. The seats in a cockpit.

Bend Any knot used to fasten two ropes together, or to secure a rope to an eye or spar, etc, which may also be easily cast off.

Bend, to To tie anything or make it fast. To bend a sail is to secure it to a yard or gaff; to bend on sheets or halyards is to make them fast to sails, spars, etc.

Bending shackle The anchor shackle (see p 10).

Bends The thick strong side strakes near a wooden ship's waterline.

Bends and hitches Collective term applied to that part of seamanship which includes the various methods of securing ropes.

Beneaped This term is used of a vessel that has gone aground at high water, and remains there if the succeeding high tide should not be high enough to refloat her.

Bent timbers The ribs of a boat.

Bermudian rig A modern racing rig in which the mainsail is tall and triangular with no throat or gaff. The head of the sail goes to the mast-head and the foot to a boom, while the luff is kept to the mast by grooving the luffrope, or by runners in a slide track. It has been incorporated in many one design classes, and is now a feature of many other rigs.

Berth Any place in a harbour allotted for the accommodation of a vessel. Place a vessel in any allotted position. A sleeping place or specified cabin in any vessel.

Berthon A small collapsible canvas boat.

Between guns A racing term for the period before a sailing race from the warning gun to the starting gun.

Between wind and water That part of a ship's side which is covered

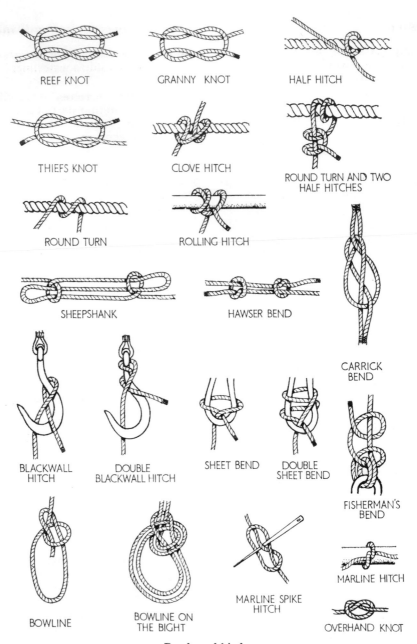

REEF KNOT

GRANNY KNOT

HALF HITCH

THIEFS KNOT

CLOVE HITCH

ROUND TURN AND TWO
HALF HITCHES

ROUND TURN

ROLLING HITCH

SHEEPSHANK

HAWSER BEND

CARRICK
BEND

BLACKWALL
HITCH

DOUBLE
BLACKWALL HITCH

SHEET BEND

DOUBLE
SHEET BEND

FISHERMAN'S
BEND

BOWLINE

BOWLINE ON
THE BIGHT

MARLINE SPIKE
HITCH

MARLINE HITCH

OVERHAND KNOT

Bends and hitches

and uncovered by continuous waves. Any vulnerable spot.

Bibbs Wooden supports on a mast for the trestle-trees. The hounds.

Bid hook A small boathook (see p 24).

Bigelow A special light flexible boom used in sailing, to which a curve is imparted by a wire and strut.

Bight A bend or loop in a rope. Any portion of rope, canvas, etc, that hangs slack between any two points.

Bilge The rounded part of a hull where the side and bottom plates meet. The flattest part of a ship's bottom internally, used for draining purposes, is called the 'bilges', as it lies between them. The widest part of a cask. Absolute nonsense.

Bilge blocks Supports placed at the bilges when a ship docks.

Bilge keel In large ships these are projecting fin-like plates, fastened outside the bilges to obtain increased steadiness. In small boats they are made of wood and fitted with 'hand-holds' in case of capsizing.

Bilge keelson A stringer placed across the frames at the bilge.

Bilge water All waste liquid that seeps down or is led to the bilges.

Bilge water alarm Any practical contrivance that will give an alarm when the bilge water rises above a predetermined level.

Bilge ways The supporting timbers for the bilge during construction.

Bilged When a vessel takes the ground in such a manner as to cause her bilges to 'spring a leak', or when she is 'stove in' near the bilge.

Bill The point of a hook. The pointed end of the fluke of an anchor.

Billboard A sloping platform for stowing an anchor at the ship's side.

Billow The surge of a large wave swelled by the wind.

Binding strakes Thick planks fitted on deck between hatchways.

Binnacle The stand or case in which the compass is housed.

Bird's nest Any lookout position aloft smaller than a crow's nest. A kink in a strand of wire rope (or nylon fishing line tangle).

Bite An anchor is said to bite when it effectually holds ground.

Bitt Fasten at or secure to the bitts.

Bitt heads The upper parts of the bitts.

Bitter end   The inboard end of the cable when made fast to the bitts; hence 'to the bitter end'—all in use and none spare or in reserve.

Bitts   Special stout vertical timbers or iron heads to which the cable or mooring rope is passed or secured.

Bitts compressor, Bitts stopper Used to hold the outboard end of the cable while securing the inboard part to the bitts.

Black ball, one   The daylight substitute for the riding light.

Black balls, two   Hoisted vertically, 6ft apart, they are the general signal used to indicate 'not under control'.

Blackwall hitch   A simple method of quickly attaching a rope to a hook. A bight is passed round the neck of the hook and the two parts are crossed, the riding or working part jamming the other. A double hitch is formed by first taking a round turn above the neck, and then crossing the ends as above.

Blade   The broad flat end of an oar; the edge that cuts into the water is the 'leading edge', the other is the 'trailing edge'. The spiral curved cutting fin of a propeller.

Blake slip stopper   A steel slip secured to the deck near the line of a chain cable, and used to hold the outboard cable.

Blanket   Take the wind of a vessel by passing close to windward of her.

Bleed a buoy   Let out water that has seeped into a buoy.

Blind bucklers   Covering plates for the hawse holes.

Blizzard   A snowstorm. Any strong wind accompanied by snow.

Block   A pulley, with one or more grooved sheaves, used to gain a mechanical advantage or to lead a rope in any required direction. It is measured by the length of its shell, and usually designated by type, shape, and number of sheaves.

Block and tackle   Mechanical device on the principle of the pulley, used for hauling and lifting, by means of various combinations of ropes and blocks to increase the applied power (see p 163).

Block stopper   A short rope attached to a block for use as a stopper when required to prevent the fall from running.

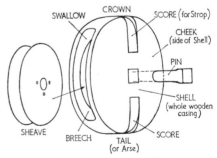

Parts of a common block

Blow, Blow up A sudden increase in the strength of the wind.

Blue ensign The ensign of HM Naval Reserve and vessels auxiliary to the RN; it may be worn by merchant vessels only when a warrant is issued by the Admiralty.

Blue Peter A blue flag with a white rectangular centre, flown as an indication that a ship is about to sail or will do so within the next 24 hours. Often used as a preparatory time signal before a sailing race, being hoisted with, or representing, the 5 minute gun.

Blue pigeon The sounding lead.

Blue riband The open ocean. A title awarded to the vessel that has made the fastest time between two points across an ocean.

Blue water The open sea, as opposed to coastal waters.

Blue water cruising Indicates the interests of those yachtsmen who take their boats farther than their local waters.

Blue-back Name applied to any one of a series of charts and plans of harbours, prepared for the use of those who cruise around our coastal waters. They are not an Admiralty publication.

Bluff A high steep bank or coast.

Bluff bows Broad raised bows with a blunt rounded entry.

Bluff-headed Term applied to a vessel whose stem is 'straight-up'.

Blunt end The stern, as opposed to the bows or 'thin end'.

Board The side of a ship. The distance between successive tacks when close hauled is often referred to as a long or short board.

Board a tack Haul on the tack tackle to bowse the tack right down.

Board, to To put foot over the side on to any vessel. 'Boarding a vessel' signifies making an entry by any means, with or without force. A group of boarders constitutes a 'boarding party'.

Boat A small open vessel constructed by man, having stability and buoyancy, and able to transfer beings and articles across water, though unsuitable for voyages to sea.

Boat ahoy The correct call used to hail a boat.

Boat boom A long spar swung outboard from a fitting on the ship's side; it is fitted with boatropes and ladders for the use of boats' crews. Boats are secured to it when not in use, and are thus kept clear of the ship's side. Frequently referred to as 'the lower boom'.

Boat chocks, boat cradles Shaped supports in which a boat rests on deck.

Boat pulling The term used for rowing when carried out for exercise, practising for regattas, or as part of any training.

Boat your oars Order given to unship the oars and lay them fore and aft within the boat.

Boathook A long stave with a hook affixed at one end, used for fending off or holding a boat alongside, or recovering anything, etc.

Boating The art of rowing, sailing, or otherwise handling a boat.

Boatrope Any rope provided for a boat to ride by. A rope from forward to a lower boom for boats to be secured by, or to a gangway where it may be lowered for the use of any boat coming alongside.

Boat's bag A handy canvas bag carried in small boats to hold important 'ready-use' articles, such as hammer and chisel, palm and needle, seizing wire, spunyarn, etc.

Boat's box The sealed box containing a boat's flares and rockets, together with a Very's pistol and cartridges.

Boat's lead and line A smaller edition of the hand line, usually comprising about 10 fathoms of cod line for use with a 5–7lb lead; it is marked off in feet for the first 3 fathoms in addition to the normal markings.

Boats recall The special flags or pennants allocated to individual boats which when hoisted alone are a recall signal.

Boatswain Pronounced and often written 'bo'sun'. The officer or seaman responsible for the supervision and maintenance of a ship's boats, sails, rigging, cordage, etc.

Boatswain's chair A stave of a cask or stout board, rove through at its ends by a sling, to make a seat for a man hoisted aloft.

Boatswain's chest, locker, or store The compartment reserved for stowage of blocks, tackles, ropes, canvas, spikes, etc.

Bobbing about Heaving and setting without making any way.

Bobstay The stay from the cutwater to the bowsprit to counteract the upward strain of the fore stays.

Bobstay piece A timber support at the stem under a bowsprit.

Bobtailer Any vessel possessing a cruiser-shaped stern.

Body plan A sectional diagram showing the curves of the frame, forward and aft, in a boat's construction.

Bold sheer A sheer (see p 146) where the freeboard of a vessel is low amidships and rises in a pronounced curve to bow and stern.

Bold shore A steep coast where the water deepens rapidly, enabling one to approach close in without fear of taking the ground.

Bollard A large circular iron post fixed strongly in any required position to receive ships' securing ropes. In ships they are usually set up in pairs. A vertical timber in a boat.

Bollard eye A large soft eye fitted in the end of a berthing hawser.

Bolsters Long canvas bags containing kapok or cork, fitted into small boats for additional buoyancy. Any shaped timber or canvas pads used to lessen the chafing of a rope.

Bolt A roll of canvas (length approx 39yd).

Boltrope The rope sewn on to the edges of sails to prevent fraying or tearing; it is fitted to the port side of all fore-and-aft sails and to the after edge of square sails, and may also be named according to the edge it is fitted to—headrope, footrope, etc.

Bone in her teeth, a Said of any vessel that produces a large quantity of foam when under way.

Bonnet A piece fastened to the foot of a sail to gather extra wind. A cover for the navel pipe (see p 118).

Booby hatch A sliding top or covered entrance to a ladder leading down to the cabin of a small boat.

Boom A spar used to extend the foot of a sail. Any spar heeled out from the ship's side, for boats, sounding, side screens, etc.

Boom horse A small iron band for fitting to a boom; it contains a small iron horse for the block of the sheets to travel on.

Boomkin A small boom. Fore tacks may be hauled down to one fitted to the bows, and mizzen sheets secured to one fitted to the stern.

Booms The spar deck or elevated structure where spare booms, spars, and light boats are stowed.

Boot top Ship's side plating between light and load waterlines.

Boot topping Special protective composition applied to the boot top.

Born weak Scornful term for any vessel feebly constructed.

Borrowing Setting a course that would normally be unsafe but which may be used with safety owing to the favourable action of the wind and tide.

Bo'sun   The abbreviation for boatswain (see p 24).

Bottle screw   A screw-threaded frame which turns on two threaded pins, each pin being fitted with an eye; used as a quick way of setting up rigging, guard rails, etc.

Bottom   The keel of a ship, hence the ship itself; often applied to all that exterior part of a ship below the waterline. The sea bed.

Bottom boards   Wooden boards and battens shaped and fitted inside the bottom of pulling boats, to keep the weight from the planking while providing a walking surface between the thwarts.

Bottom line, hogging line   A length of chain placed under a vessel from side to side.

Bound   Proceeding to any special place, in any special direction, or for any particular purpose.

Bow   The stem. The fore end itself. The bow of a shackle is the rounded part at the opposite end to the jaws.

Bow line   The hawser securing the bows to a jetty, etc. A headfast.

Bow sheets, headsheets   The

floorboards, benches, and space in the fore part of a boat.

Bow wave   The picturesque wave on each bow as the stem of a ship cuts through the water at high speed.

Bower anchor   The main anchor of a vessel, used with chain cable.

Bowline   A knot used to tie a loop or bight in a rope, the large loop being held by two small interlocking bights, making it easy to undo. A bridle used on a course (see p 48) for hauling the leech forward.

Bowline on the bight   A useful type of bowline for slinging a man, having a large double loop that may be adjusted and formed with one part bigger than the other. The large loop is used for the seat and the small one under the arms, while the knot is held in front of the man.

Bowman   The foremost man of a boat's crew; he pulls the bow oar, or tends the tack, boathook, painter, towrope, etc.

Bows   The ship's side at the foremost part. A warning order given in a boat when going alongside for the bowman to ship his oar and man his boathook.

Bows on   Said of a vessel approaching from any direction when her fore-and-aft line points to the observer. Keeping the bow pointed to any object.

Bowse, bouse To pull down on a rope. To 'bowse taut' is to haul down taut.

Bowsprit A spar projecting from the bow of a sailing vessel, to which the headsails are secured.

Box off Pay off from a wind that has shifted ahead, or, if a ship has come too close, clewing out the fore-sail to windward.

Box the compass Name all the consecutive points or quarter points all round the compass. A description applied to anyone or anything that turns full circle.

Boxhauling A method used to get out of a tight spot when a vessel misses stays and has insufficient room in which to ware; the headsails are extended so as to veer her sharp round on her heel. In square-rigged ships headyards are put flat aback and their sheets hauled to windward.

Boxwood scale The graduated scale on which the used sounding tube is laid for reading off the depth.

Brace A rope used to trim a yard in square-rigged ships; there are two to each yard, secured near the yard arms, so as to obtain maximum horizontal trim. When 'on a wind' with yards trimmed near a fore-and-aft direction, both yards and ship are said to be 'braced up'; when running, with yards athwartships,

both are referred to as being 'braced in'.

Brail up Spill the wind from a sail by using brails.

Brails Ropes fitted for trussing or gathering a sail to spill the wind.

Break A part of the ship where it joins another at a different level. A flag hoisted in a roll within a bow-knot is broken when it is jerked loose at a certain time. This practice is never used with ensigns. A sail put up 'in stops' may also be broken.

Break ground Heave an anchor out of the ground.

Break her back A vessel may do this when so shaken or loosened that her frame droops at both ends. When her keel is thus out of alignment, her 'back is broken'.

Break her sheer Opposite to 'keeping her sheer' (see p 99).

Break off A vessel close hauled and on her course, being 'headed' by a wind that compels her to sail to leeward, is said to 'break off'; the action of the wind is said to 'break her off'.

Break tacks Go from one tack to the other.

Breaker A large wave that curls and breaks on a shore. A small cask.

27

Breaking strain, breaking load When tabulated details are not to hand, a quick reliable way to assess the breaking load of hemp, manilla, or sisal is to square the circumference in inches and divide by three, the result being a good safety margin in tons. The normal 'working load' is accepted as one-sixth of this.

Breakwater A structure of masonry, rock, etc, constructed to form a wall to provide protection and shelter in an artificial harbour. A protective metal barrier erected athwartships on a deck to break the force of any seas that are shipped.

Breast, breastfast, breastrope A hawser from any part of a ship to a jetty, being led approximately at right angles to the ship's side.

Breast band The wide band of sennit affixed above the apron (see p 11) in the chains for the support of the leadsman when 'heaving the lead' (see p 88); sometimes called the breastrope.

Breast hook A selected 'crook' of wood shaped as a knee and fitted to hold the gunwales and apron firmly to a boat's stem.

Breast off Move a vessel from alongside in a sideways movement.

Breastwork The rails and stanchions placed athwartships to separate any part of a deck, or to safeguard

the end of a superstructure. Any ornamentation affixed thereto.

Breech That part of a block opposite the swallow. A rope is rove through the swallow but it cannot be rove through the breech.

Breeches buoy A circular lifebuoy fitted with canvas breeches suitable to hold a person; it is part of the lifesaving apparatus used to transfer persons from vessels wrecked close inshore, etc.

Breeze A wind varying from light to strong.

Bridge The raised platform with a clear view all round from which the captain controls the ship.

Bridle A length of rope secured at both ends and controlled from its centre. A vessel riding to two anchors is said to ride on a bridle; when secured to a buoy, the cable from the hawse to the buoy becomes a bridle.

Brig A two-masted sailing vessel having square sails on both masts and a gaff mainsail.

Brigantine A two-masted sailing vessel with square sails on the foremast and schooner rig on the main.

Bring by the lee Alter course to leeward when running, so that the lee side is suddenly brought to windward. The main boom must be

28

carefully tended (see **Accidental gybe**, p 7).

Bring home the anchor   When the anchor is being weighed and the flukes yield to allow the anchor to be dragged to the ship instead of vice versa, it is termed 'bringing home' the anchor.

Bring home the log   Recover and set up the logship when the pin slips.

Bring to   Check the way of a ship. Luff and bring her up into the wind. Lead a rope to a capstan or winch drum, take turns, and back it up.

Bring up   Stop. Anchor, moor, or secure to a buoy.

Bring up with a round turn   Snub. Stop something or someone abruptly.

Bristol fashion   A vessel is 'all shipshape and Bristol fashion' when attaining perfection in cleanliness, smartness, efficiency, and appearance.

Broach   Open or break in on a cargo, or make a hole in a cask, whether lawfully or to pilfer.

Broach to   In stormy seas with the wind aft a boat may tend to slew round against her helm, thus putting her sails aback and endangering the masts, with the possible risk of being turned 'broadside on' to the sea.

Broad on the bow   Said of an object that bears a little farther aft than 45° (which is 'on the bow'), this being an approximation.

Broad pennant   A swallow-tail burgee flown by a commodore.

Broad reach   Sailing a reach with the wind just abaft the beam.

Broadside on, broadside to   Sideways on to.

Broken back   The quality of a ship when hogged excessively so that she appears arched (see **Break her back**, p 27).

Brought to   Said of any cable or rope when led to a capstan or any bollards, etc, and taken round them.

Brought up   Arrived at. Applied to a vessel whose way is stopped by any method. Anchored, or moored, the ship having 'got her cable'.

Brought up all standing   The sudden stoppage of a ship's way without reducing sail or power, eg by a sudden change of wind, or striking an object, submerged or otherwise.

Brow   A narrow portable gangway from ship to shore.

Buck the wind   Sail out in face of strong head winds.

Bucketing Jerky rowing. Dipping an oar in and out of the water without pulling it right through the stroke.

Builders measurements (BM) A method adopted for calculating the tonnage of yachts according to their load waterline (see **Loadline,** p 107).

Built mast One that has been made from more than one tree or piece of timber.

Bulb and plate Old method of yacht design with fin keel and lead bulb.

Bulb-keeler A sailing boat with a heavy bulb-shaped keel.

Bulkhead Any transverse or longitudinal vertical partition maintaining rigidity of construction and dividing a vessel into watertight compartments.

Bull ring, Panama lead A large circular steel ring fitted transversely on the bow as a fairlead for head-ropes or towing hawser.

Bulldog grip A U-shaped steel bow with threaded ends, over which a bridge is placed and clamped down by nuts; used to hold or bind two wires together. The U-piece should always be fitted over the loose end and not over the standing part.

Bullivant's nippers Steel appli-

ances in various sizes for temporarily holding a wire under great stress.

Bullrope A rope from the bowsprit to a buoy to keep it clear of a vessel's stem in slack water.

Bull's eye A wooden block or fair-lead grooved to take a strop but without a sheave, having a hole bored in it to take a rope. A piece of thick glass let into the deck to provide light below.

Bullwanger A strop on a yard, to which a sail may be lashed.

Bulwarks The sides of a ship above the upper deck; formerly for defence purposes, they form a protection from the sea and also prevent things falling overboard.

Bumboat A small flat-bottomed boat used by local traders for selling their merchandise to crews of ships lying off shore.

Bumpkin A boomkin (see p 25).

Bunt The middle portion of a sail, net, or bag.

Bunting Light worsted material used for making flags, pennants, etc. Collective term for flags or similar decorations.

Bunting tosser A signalman.

Buntline A rope passing from the

footrope to the mast and thence led to the deck, to assist in hauling up square sails.

Buoy A floating structure anchored on the sea bed. Buoys are divided into two main classes—as navigational aids and for mooring ships.

Buoyage A system of buoys laid out to mark a fairway for shipping.

Buoyancy Ability to float, expressed as positive or negative.

Buoyancy bags Air bags fitted in small boats for additional buoyancy.

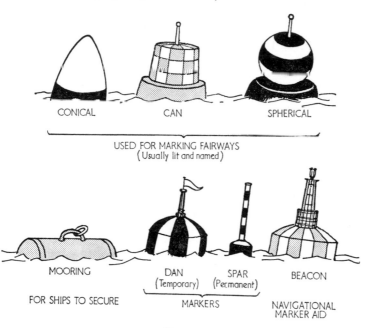

CONICAL   CAN   SPHERICAL

USED FOR MARKING FAIRWAYS
(Usually lit and named)

MOORING   DAN (Temporary)   SPAR (Permanent)   BEACON

FOR SHIPS TO SECURE   MARKERS   NAVIGATIONAL MARKER AID

Buoys

Buoy is watching, the Remarked of a buoy that is visibly floating and fulfilling its purpose.

Buoy rope Any rope used to mark anything on the bottom by a floating marker (it should be strong enough to retrieve if necessary).

Buoyancy tanks Sealed air containers of various shapes and sizes, specially fitted within a boat to provide buoyancy.

Buoyancy test Placing all gear and the crew within a boat, and filling it with sea water to ascertain the buoyancy.

Burden, burthen　The carrying capacity of a ship.

Burgee　A swallow-tail flag. Frequently applied to a triangular flag indicating the owner, or a club flag used by members.

Burton　A type of purchase (see **Tackles**, p 163).

Butt　The ends of planks, plates, etc. Place end to end. The largest end of a spar or piece of timber. A large cask.

Butt sling　A length of rope for use when slinging a cask.

Butt strap　A strip of wood or plating covering two pieces joined at their butts, for both strengthening and protection.

Butter box　An awkwardly built boat with excessive beam and top-hamper.

Butterfly block　A small snatch block fitted with a strop and a long tail for affixing it where it may be required for use.

Butterfly nuts　Hand-tightening wing nuts as used on watertight hatches.

Buttock　The under part of the

rounded overhang of a ship's stern.

Buttock lines　Lines used in boat-building plans to represent fore-and-aft vertical sections equidistant from the hull centreline.

By and large　With the wind near the beam. 'By the wind' and 'sailing large' signify that the wind is before or just abaft the beam respectively; thus the terms indicate a little of each, or a happy medium. It also implies taking the rough with the smooth, and is thus used in the sense of 'broadly speaking, all things considered'.

By the board　Anything handed, thrown, or fallen over the ship's side. Said of a mast that breaks off close to the deck; hence the term 'gone by the board', meaning lost or of no further use.

By the head　Applied to a vessel whose ballast is stowed too far forward or whose bows set lower in the water than normally.

By the lee　Said of a boat when the wind comes on the same side as she is carrying her mainsail (see **Bring by the lee**, p 28).

By the mark　The phrase prefixed to a sounding, as reported by the leadsman when one of the marks on the line is at water level while the line is vertical.

By the stern Opposite to 'by the head'.

By the wind Close hauled. As a general term, to within about six points of the wind.

By-points Those points of the compass between the intermediates, and the cardinals and half cardinals. There are sixteen, easily remembered as they contain the word 'by', eg north by east.

Cabin cruiser A motor boat with cabin and berths, for private cruises.

Cable The chain or rope to which the anchor is shackled or secured, varying in size according to the type of ship. A nautical short distance measurement of one-tenth of a mile, roughly 200yd.

Cable Clench Clinch bolt (see p 41).

Cable holder A drum, fitted with sprockets to receive the chain cable, placed on deck near the navel pipe, and used to heave in or veer when working cable; it may be geared to work with the capstan or worked independently.

Cable laid A term applied to any large hawser made up from three or four hawser laid ropes, which are laid up the opposite way to their own lay; thus four right-handed ropes will make up into a left-handed cable laid rope.

Caboose Freely pronounced 'caboosh'. The galley. Any small deckhouse. Any odd corner of a ship fitted out and used as a store.

Cairn A mound of stones erected prominently as a landmark.

Caisson Pronounced 'cassoon'. A watertight structure used as a wall to close an entrance to a dock, being floated in or out of position and flooded when in use.

Calcium light A small canister containing calcium, and fitted with an easy tear-away pin. It is bound to a lifebuoy, and the pin secured to the ship by a stray line. When the buoy is removed for use, the pin is torn away, leaving a hole for water to enter the container when thrown overboard, thus showing its position by smoke in daylight and by flame during darkness.

Call sign A distinguishing signal-group of four letters allotted to every vessel for identification.

Calliper hooks (also called **clip, clasp, clip-match, clove** or **sister hooks**) A pair of flat overlapping hooks on one ring, each facing opposite directions; when closed together, they form one eye.

Calm An unruffled sea with absence of wind. Quiet.

c

Camber A small dock where ships may load or unload. A sloping slipway for the hauling up of vessels. The curve of a plank, or of a deck so that water may run off.

Camel A large hollow vessel of wood or metal, used to obtain buoyancy in lifting a ship. Generally used in pairs during salvage operations, they are sunk and placed in position under a ship to be raised, and rise as the water is pumped from them.

Can buoy A buoy that shows a flat top above water; when painted red, or red and white chequered, it denotes the port hand of a channel when tide is flooding.

Canoe A long narrow light portable rowing craft, propelled by the use of paddles; canoes vary from the primitive dug-out to a canvas-covered frame, and are now expertly designed for sailing.

Canopy A canvas covering on a metal frame, or supported by stanchions, for protecting hatchways.

Cant Tilt or lean anything. The 'cant line' is the groove between strands of a rope, rows of casks, etc.

Canvas A coarse fabric made of flax, obtainable from a stout quality (No oo) to very fine (No 10), and supplied in 'bolts' (rolls); used for making sails, awnings, screens, etc. A general term to indicate all a ship's sails.

Cap A fitting over the head of a mast for retaining the next mast above it.

Cap a rope Protect the end of a rope by covering it with a canvas 'dolly' and whipping it back.

Cappen The thin wood covering around a boat atop the gunwale.

Capsize Turn over (a boat, or a coil of rope ready for running).

Capstan A revolving bollard supplied for lifting anchors and working cables, or drawing a ship to a jetty by hawsers.

Capstan bars Stout wooden bars inserted into the capstan by means of iron shoes, to work it by hand.

Captain The senior officer in charge of a ship.

Cardinal points The four main points of the compass—north, east, south, and west.

Careen Place a vessel on her side so that work may be carried out on her underwater parts.

Carley raft or **float** A specially constructed float for lifesaving purposes, consisting of a large oval-shaped light metal frame with sufficient buoyancy to support a number of people in it.

Carlins   Short fore-and-aft timbers between beams.

Carpenters stopper   A portable metal clamp and wedge, fitted to two chains; it is shackled to an eyebolt on the deck and used to hold any wire.

Carrick bend   The method used for joining two hawsers that are required to round the capstan.

Carry away   The breaking of any spar, or parting of any rope or fitting.

Carry her way   To cover a long distance before stopping after heading into the wind or switching off engine, or when she goes about and sails easily round on to a new tack.

Carrying helm or **rudder**   Term used when for any reason a small angle of helm or rudder is necessary to counteract any continuous inclination to wander off course.

Carvel-built   A boat constructed with its planking laid edge to edge on a very stout framework, thus making smooth surfaced sides.

Carving note   The official authorisation, after the survey of a ship, to mark her with her name, tonnage, and port.

Case   In diagonal-built boats the inner planking.

Casing   Sheet metal framing any enclosure to give protection; usually named after the purpose for which it is erected, eg funnel casing.

Cast   Point a ship when getting under way, so that she may fill on the requisite tack. Take a sounding. Throw off.

Cast an anchor   Drop or let go an anchor; the term is obsolescent.

Cast loose   Said of anything unwieldy that breaks away from its lashings, etc. It is said to 'take charge' when dangerous.

Cast off   Loosen from. Let go hawsers if secured alongside.

Cat   A widely used term for a boat of any description.

Cat boat   A beamy small boat, cat-rigged (see below).

Cat davit   A special davit fitted for use in catting the anchor.

Cat head   A strong beam or metal support fitted to project from the bow, to take the large block used when catting the anchor.

Cat holes   Openings in the stern for leading out stern-fasts.

Cat pennant   The rope used to lift the anchor to the cat head.

Cat rig A large fore-and-aft sail, gaffed and boomed, hoisted on a stout mast stepped right forward. Useful in calm waters.

Cat the anchor Hoist the anchor to the cat head instead of the hawse pipe, where it is hung by a slip over the bow; this is frequently resorted to when the cable has to be broken and used as a bridle when securing to a buoy.

Catamaran A boat or raft, with more than one hull or keel joined together by beams, which sails exceptionally well. A large wooden platform used as a floating fender or stage.

Catch anchor A kedge anchor (see p 99).

Catch a turn Take a quick turn with a rope round the nearest pin or cleat, so as to take the weight temporarily.

Catching a crab A fault in rowing when the blade of an oar enters the water incorrectly and is forced down to become out of control, so that it is swept aft and jams, often resulting in the oarsman being capsized back over his thwart.

Catenary The length of cable used to form the centre part of a long tow, where it helps withstand any sudden stress.

Cat-rigged schooner A two-masted vessel with no jibs, her foremast set right up in the bows.

Catspaw A twist put in the bight of a rope, forming two loops to take a hook. A light puff of wind, strong enough to be of some advantage to an alert helmsman when sailing.

Caulking Driving oakum into the seams of planking, or decks, to make them watertight before 'paying' them with pitch. Any substance used for this purpose.

Cavitation Excessive vibration caused by the incorrect size or faulty positioning of a boat's propeller.

Celestial fix A fix obtained by measuring the angle of any celestial body at a certain fixed time.

Centreboard A wooden board lowered from a sailing boat through a slot in the middle of her keel, its purpose being to help the boat sail closer to the wind and reduce leeway. It may be brought up when running, and also in shallow water. When made of metal it is called a centreplate.

Certificate of registry The form giving a ship's name, measurements, tonnage, and other constructional details, signed by a registrar. The master of a ship must ensure he has this onboard, otherwise the ship is liable to be detained.

Chafe Rub or wear away by constant usage and friction.

Chaffer A term applied to a jib shivering in the wind.

Chafing gear Matting, spunyarn, or other protection affixed to spars, rigging, etc, to reduce chafing of ropes. Chafing plates are metal fittings on coamings, etc, where sharp edges may hasten wear on ropes.

Chain cable A wrought iron chain, as used with an anchor.

Chain locker, cable locker The space below the navel pipe where the inboard end of the cable is secured and the remainder stowed.

Chain plates The metal fittings secured to the sides of a boat to which shrouds are set up (from the 'chains' of sailing ships).

Chain splice Used when splicing a rope to a chain. One strand is unlaid well back, and the two laid up parts passed through the end link; the pair are separated, and one of the two strands is laid up in the lay of the single strand not used, while the other is tucked near the link; the two strands in the same lay are finished off farther back, as in a long splice.

Chain stopper A short length of chain for use as a stopper to hold a wire under stress.

Chain swivel, swivel piece A swivel link put in cable to prevent it kinking.

Chains A ledge fixed outboard of the bulwarks, in a position just abaft a mast, for spreading and setting up the lower rigging. The special platform erected for the leadsman in ships which have no chains. A series of metal links passing one through another, used for moorings, or with an anchor in small boats; in larger vessels the large chains used are called cables.

Change trim Vary the difference between the fore and aft draughts of a vessel.

Channel The deepest part of a passage through which a main current flows. A groove to convey water, also called a channel-way.

Chapel Wear round to the original course after being taken aback; if this is caused by bad steering, the helmsman has 'built himself a chapel'.

Charlie Noble The ugly H-type iron chimney-top from a galley or stove.

Chart A detailed survey of waters and coastlines, with the relative latitude and longitude and other detailed information, represented on and as a map, and used for navigational purposes. Charts are the sailor's road maps; he should be sure to ascertain whether soundings are shown in fathoms, feet, or the metric system.

Chart datum The level to which soundings are reduced on any one chart; it is the level below which the tide is unlikely to fall, and is used for the datum line of the area on that particular chart, as the basis of the hydrographical survey.

Charted depth The height of the chart datum level above the bottom.

Charter To hire a vessel by deed of contract. A 'charter party' is the document setting out conditions and terms for the hiring.

Charthouse, chartroom The room or space set apart on or near the bridge for the stowage of charts, chronometer, etc, and for the special use of the navigator.

Chartwork The art of coastal navigation by reference to charts.

Check Ease out a rope carefully in small amounts, while at the same time keeping the strain.

Cheek block A sheave that is pinned to or set against a boom or spar, having but one cheek holding the pin.

Cheeks The sides of a block. Knee pieces affixed to a mast to support the cross trees.

Cheese down Coil a rope-end to an ornamental flat finish, by centring the end and turning it, keeping all parts close to each other flat on deck.

Cheese cutter A type of drop keel.

Chequered Refers to any flag, buoy, etc, displaying a pattern of squares in two different colours.

Cherub log A type of patent log incorporating a rotator towed astern to register speed and distance.

Chess trees Wooden spurs fitted with a sheave at their ends, and secured in position. A tack is hauled down to them to 'board' it.

Chimes A bevelled channel in the waterways of sailing ships.

Chine The intersection of the straight sides with the flat bottom planks of a boat.

Chinese windlass A machine with two different size drums: a rope is brought to the large one to heave in, while the small drum veers the other part, a block being in the bight.

Chinkle A small loop formed in a rope or line.

Chinse Stop the seams of boats with oakum or cotton yarn.

Chock An adjectival prefix meaning as close or as full as possible, eg chock full, chock forward. A wedge. Wedge so as to prevent movement. A fairlead.

Chock a block Said when the two blocks of a tackle are so close together that no further purchase is possible, or when anything is hauled hard up to a block. Full to capacity.

Choke a luff A temporary measure whereby the bight of the hauling part of a tackle is jammed under the sheave of its neighbouring part, to hold it and prevent it 'walking back'.

Choppy Said of the sea when the surface is irregular but not rough.

Christening A special ceremony for naming a ship at her launching.

Chronometer The ship's timepiece, carried specially for navigational purposes. It is set in a safe place mounted in gymbals, and records the time exceptionally accurately.

Chummy ships Ships or boats which through circumstances are continuously together, and whose crews are friendly.

Circumnavigate Sail round.

Clamp A plank fitted on the inside of a ship's frame to act as a bearer for a beam or joint. A hinged half-circular metal band used to secure booms, derricks, etc, in their stowage.

Clap on A call to give a hand to help when a rope is being hauled. To 'clap on more canvas' is to make more sail.

Clapper A chafing piece in the jaws of a gaff.

Class boats Boats that are specially built to conform to a certain formula and design, their features being similar to others in that particular class. There are numerous named classes, especially among the popular racing dinghy types, each class having its own distinctive sailmarking.

Class flag Flag broken at a club masthead as a warning 10 minutes to the start of a class boat race (a gun or other prearranged signal may be used to draw attention to this).

Claw ring A metal ring, shaped like callipers, which fits loosely round a boom; used with roller reefing gear.

Claw to windward Beat up gradually to windward from any danger spot or from a lee shore; this is usually termed 'clawing off'.

Clear Empty, unload, escape. Opposite to foul. Sail by and past anything such as a cape, rock, buoy, etc.

Clear ahead or **astern** When no part of a boat crosses another boat's hull or equipment.

Clear anchor A report given to the bridge when weighing anchor to indicate that it has been sighted and is not foul of any obstruction.

Clear another boat's wind To keep sufficient distance so as to be safe from leebowing.

Clear berth Sufficient space for a vessel to swing when at anchor, with no possibility of fouling anything.

Clear for running Said of a rope that has been coiled down and then capsized, to enable the working part to run off freely.

Clear hawse Open hawse (see p 121).

Clear hawse slip A special slip fitted with a roller shackle, used to clear a foul hawse. It is lowered over by a rope rove through the roller, and put on the cable below the part that is fouled; it is then hove in, the cable broken, turns taken out, reshackled, and both cables veered to ride at open hawse.

Clear lower deck A call meaning 'all hands on deck'.

Clear the board Remove all obstructions; make a clean sweep.

Clear the land Attain a position with no possibility of being endangered by reefs, shoals, etc.

Clear view screen A rotating circular glass disc fitted in a position to give clear vision in any weather.

Clearing line A line drawn on a chart to mark off a course giving a margin of safety clear of an obstruction.

Clearing mark An object shown on a chart which, with another such mark, may be joined to produce a clearing line.

Cleat A wood or metal fitting with two arms, or horns, to which a rope may be belayed.

Clench Fasten a rivet or nail (clench bolt), by beating and then burring its end over a roove (see p 136) with a hammer (see **Clinch** below).

Clench-built Clinker-built (see below).

Clew In fore-and-aft sails, the after lower corner; in square sails, either lower corner, the forward one being the weather one when in use. Comprehensively it refers to all four corners of any sail.

Clew garnet A small tackle used for hauling up the clew of a course to a yard, for furling. 'Clew lines' are ropes used for the same purpose on the upper square sails.

Clew up Truss sails up to the yards. End or finish off.

Clinch Join and fasten two overlapping strakes by passing a rivet through the overlap and clenching it. Fix finally, or firmly. Clinch and clench are practically synonymous.

Clinch bolt, clench bolt The fitting at the bottom of the cable locker, for securing the inboard end of the cable. A copper rivet.

Clinker-built A boat so constructed that each plank is clenched in position, overlapping the one below it.

Clinometer, inclinometer Any instrument, or simple pendulum and graduated arc, fitted to show the angle of heel during a list, or, if turned fore and aft, the angle of pitch.

Clipper A fast sailing ship with fine lines, raked masts, and sharp bows.

Clipper bow A bow whose stem curves inward of a line from the stem head to the waterline. An outward curve gives a 'spoon bow'.

Close Narrow any distance by coming nearer. To 'close the land' is to approach it from seaward.

Close aboard Almost touching. Near to anything referred to.

Close harbour An artificially enclosed harbour as distinct from one that is a natural formation.

Close hauled Sailing as close to the wind as possible, or within four to six points of it.

Close jammed Sailing so close on a wind as to lose its full benefit; one point off would be better.

Close linked Said of small chain that is not studded.

Close reach A fine reach (see p 66).

Close reefed Reefed down as much as possible. Dressed in oilskins for bad weather, or wearing an overcoat with all buttons and collar done up. Tightly folded up.

Close stowing anchor An anchor with a fixed stock, fitted with a balancing band for use when stowing on the anchor bed, as it cannot enter a hawse pipe. Now practically obsolete.

Close up Applied to a flag, or signal hoist, when hoisted right up. To man any special positions.

Close winded Able to sail fairly close to the wind.

Cloth A length of canvas used to form part of a sail.

Cloud cleaners Name for the imaginary sails atop the skysails.

Clove hitch A hitch used to join one rope to another or to any other object; it is formed by two half hitches, the end of the second one being brought up through its own part.

Club Any spar fitted to the foot of a triangular sail.

Club hauling A method used to extricate a ship from a dangerous position. The leeward anchor is let down, and a spring is then taken from the lee quarter and secured to the cable. By veering cable and heaving on the spring, the ship may be turned; when she is swung sufficiently to fill on the new tack, the cable is broken and a buoy attached to the spring, all of which are then slipped.

Club pennant The burgee, flag, or pennant of any yachting club— generally displayed on the bridge of a club or on the committee-boat to signify that an advertised event will take place.

Club topsail An enlarged topsail with clubs extending it; sometimes used to replace a gaff topsail.

Clubbing Drifting stern foremost in a fast running tide, sheering with

the rudder as necessary, and with the anchor dropped short, to bring a vessel to her berth.

Clubfooted Applied to any vessel built with a wide forefoot.

Clump block A short stout block having a larger swallow than a common block of similar size.

Clump cat head A strong projecting sheave for suspending an anchor by the 'catting pennant' when it is being catted or uncatted.

Coach roof The raised part of a cabin or cabin top inboard of the sides, constructed for headroom in small boats.

Coaming A vertical metal protective erection around hatches, etc, which prevents water entering or anything falling in from the deck, and to which coverings are secured to batten down. A raised wooden rail round a well or cockpit in small boats.

Coastal sea areas The division of the sea round the British coast into named areas for reference purposes, as used in weather forecasts.

Coastal quick release (CQR) An improved type of patent anchor, popular amongst yachtsmen and small boat fraternities.

Coastline The borderline where the sea meets the land.

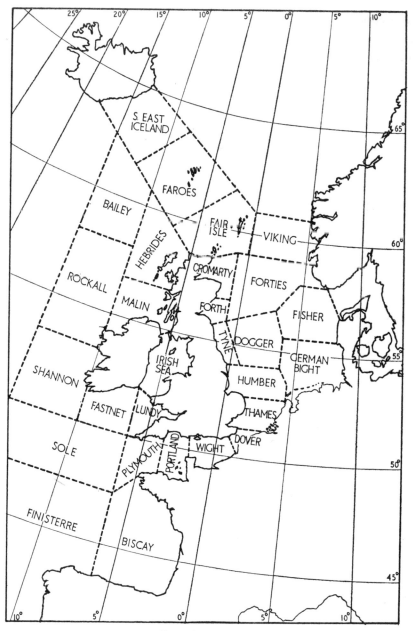

Coastal sea areas

Coble, cobble A beamy flat-bottomed boat with high prow, square stern, and often a deep rudder.

Cockbilling Suspended to swing freely (see **Acockbill**, p 7).

Cocked hat The small triangular position indicated on a chart by three positional lines that should meet at one spot but do not quite do so; the centre of the 'hat' is the point marked off.

Cockpit The after well in sailing boats, where the helmsman sits. A space on the orlop deck of old ships, used as a sick bay.

Code pendant Used to indicate that the International Code of Signals is being used, and also as the 'answering' pennant. It is red, with two white vertical bars.

Cod line Small eighteen-thread line used for many handy purposes such as lacings, bending on sails, ornamental knots, etc; it is supplied for fishing, and is one size larger than mackerel line.

Codshead and mackerel-tail A description applied to sailing yachts designed with bluff bows and a long run aft, the greatest beam being forward.

Cofferdam A watertight structure used in building piers, etc. A separating compartment built in for insulating purposes.

Coil Rope made up in circular form, usually supplied in 113 fathom lengths, irrespective of size. Any rope or part of a rope when formed into rings, each one lying over another, within a small space; each of the rings is a coil, or 'fake'.

Coil, to To coil a rope, start by working from the fixed end to the loose end, and take natural turns, called fakes, by forming rings of convenient size, each one over the preceding one; on completion the whole coil is capsized, and neatly arranged so as to be ready to run out free. Right-handed rope is coiled clockwise, left-handed anticlockwise.

Coir Grass line or rope.

Collapsible Name given to any light craft with strong frames covered by fabric and capable of being easily folded.

Collar knot A knot used for rigging jury shrouds. Two long ropes are centred and their bights joined by a granny knot, which is kept open and passed over the masthead down on to the hounds; this leaves two ends each side for setting up.

Collision The impact of two vessels under way, or in motion. Correctly speaking it should not refer to the hitting of any stationary object, ashore or afloat.

Collision bulkheads Strong transverse bulkheads fitted near the stem and stern, which should always be kept watertight at sea.

Collision mat A large special mat threaded with thrums (see p 164) or any sail, tarpaulin, or similar article, kept available for placing outboard over the damaged part after a collision. It is placed in position by a 'lowering line', hauled down by the 'bottom line', passed under the ship, and retained in place by two 'fore-and-afters'.

Collision stations A prepared plan which includes details for ensuring the closing of watertight doors, fanshafts, etc, placing the mat, turning out boats, and standing by rafts and lifebelts; details of the plan should be known and exercised by all hands.

Colours Name given to a ship's national ensign. Colours are hoisted at 0800 in summer and at 0900 in winter on ships in harbour, and hauled down daily at sunset. Colours are not lowered at sunset by ships at sea, but remain hoisted.

Comb cleats Double-arched bridge cleats, also used as fairleads or bee blocks.

Combers Large seas or breakers.

Come to A ship is said to 'come to' when she flies up nearer to the wind.

Come to anchor To ease speed, cast an anchor, and ride by it. It is preferable to come to anchor on the tack that will stem the tide, where the wind is across the stream.

Come up with Overhaul another vessel or person. Meet.

Coming home Said of an anchor that doesn't hold the ground, and heaves in towards the ship instead of 'biting'.

Coming inboard An expression used of anything approaching a ship that will hit her.

Coming on Refers to tides when they increase daily, ie during the period from neaps to springs.

Coming over A warning shout given by the helmsman of a sailing boat to his crew when the boom is about to swing over in a gybe.

Commander A large wooden mallet used in rigging work.

Commission To place a ship in a state of readiness for service.

Commodore The senior member of any yacht, boating, or similar club.

Common bend Name given to the ordinary single sheet bend, usually when the end is rove through rope and not through a thimble.

45

Common block The ordinary plain wooden pulley block.

Common whipping Used to bind the end of a rope to prevent it from unlaying and fraying; made with sailmaker's twine, or with stronger line on large ropes. After the first two turns have been jammed over the end, it is passed round and round tightly and close together, the end being tucked under the last few turns.

Companion way or **ladder** A ladder leading from the deck to a cabin or saloon. Any wide ladder with hand-rails or manropes.

Compass An instrument used to indicate position relative to a meridian. It comprises a magnetic needle or needles and a graduated card within a bowl mounted on gymbals, and is housed in a 'binnacle' (see also **Gyro compass**, p 83).

Compass bearing The position of any object observed, as indicated by the compass.

Compass card The circular card, usually of mica and marked off in points or degrees, to which the magnetic needles are affixed, the whole being pivoted within the compass bowl.

Compass corrector box The small box within the binnacle of a boat's compass that contains small corrector magnets.

Compass course The angle between the north and south line of a magnetic compass and the fore-and-aft line of a ship.

Compass error The amount a compass is deflected by the joint effect of variation and deviation.

Compass pivot The needle point in the centre of a compass bowl; it is tipped with iridium so that the card may rotate freely.

Compass rose A graduated circle printed on a chart for use as a reference to show the true and magnetic north.

Complain A ship is said to do this when she is creaking.

Complimentary ensign When entering a foreign port, it is an act of courtesy to hoist the ensign of that country on the foremast.

Composite vessel A vessel constructed with a metal frame, but with the planking on it made of wooden not metal plates.

Compressor A pivoted iron bar or arm, fitted at the lower end of a navel pipe or at the foot of the bitts, to snub and bowse the cable. A steel wedge fitted across the navel pipe itself that is engaged by turning a hand-wheel on deck.

Con Give the orders and direct the steering of a ship.

Concluding line The small line running through the centre of the treads of a jumping ladder, to bring them all close together.

Cone A black conical shape used for storm or distant signals.

Conical buoys Buoys showing a conical-shaped top above water. When painted black, or black and white chequered, they denote the starboard hand of a channel when the tide is flooding.

Constant bearing A bearing that remains the same, even though the ship is moving. If it refers to another ship, there is a risk of collision.

Convert Change the type or class of any boat by alterations; a distinction is usually made between amateur and professional 'conversions'.

Copings Curved ends of iron knees that hook into the beams. The name is often misapplied to coamings.

Copper captain Anyone who styles himself captain, without authority to do so.

Copper-bottomed Said of earlier ships whose hulls were sheathed with copper plates to protect them against fouling.

Coracle A small round or oval boat made of wickerwork, with a wrapping of waterproofed fabric as its skin; it can be carried by one man and is useful on lakes, canals, etc.

Cord Small rope of less than 1in circumference.

Cordage The general term embracing all ropes made from vegetable fibres.

Cork fender Usually a bag of old cork, shredded, with any kind of outer protection, and with the knot of its lanyard enclosed.

Corticene A hard-wearing deck-covering material, resembling a thick linoleum, which is glued down to iron deckplates; its brown surface can be scrubbed or polished to give a pleasing appearance.

Cotton rope A white flexible rope of low breaking strain, often used in yachts. It is more ornamental than practical.

Counter A projecting stern. The underside of the overhang of a stern.

Counter currents Currents that run in opposite directions. Currents that form under the lee counter of a ship under way, and which not only retain floating objects but are often capable of sucking a man under.

Counter rails Decorative mouldings ornamenting a vessel's counter.

Course The direction steered, or laid, from point to point; the angle between the fore-and-aft line of the ship and the meridian. The square sail bent to a lower yard, the mainsail thus being the main course, etc.

Course recorder An instrument that will manipulate a controlled plotter, thus continuously recording the position of the ship.

Court of Survey A court of experienced nautical assessors who meet to examine a vessel and ascertain her condition.

Courtesy ensign The 'complimentary ensign' (see p 46).

Cow tails Ends of an unwhipped rope that are unravelled and frayed.

Coxswain One who steers a boat. One in charge of a boat and her crew.

Crab A small winch (see also **Catching a crab**, p 36).

Crabfashion Any method of progression in an awkward sideways manner.

Crack ship Said of any vessel that is first class in all respects.

Cracking on Carrying all possible sail, or more than is safe under the circumstances, so as to increase speed.

Cradle A frame used to support a

48

boat when transporting her, hauling her up a slipway, or resting her; also a frame supporting a vessel during construction, so that she will slide down the ways in it when she is launched. A railed-in or rope-guarded stage or platform used for working over the side of a vessel in dock.

Craft Any small vessel. Any type of ship.

Cranky A description applied to any boat or ship that heels too easily.

Cranse iron A circular boom iron fitted to a bowsprit to take the stays.

Crazy Applied to any ship that is old and rotten.

Creeper A grappling iron for recovering lost wires, etc.

Crew, to To assist the helmsman in sailing boats.

Cringles Rope loops or metal thimbles fitted into the boltropes of sails at the corners. Strands of rope used to make a cringle. Those fitted in line with reef points, are 'reef cringles'.

Crinolines A bunch of steadying lines that spread out from the lower block of a purchase.

Crooks Curved pieces of timber in which the grain follows the curve.

Cross beam Any heavy timber fitted athwartships for strengthening.

Cross bearings A simultaneous observation of two separate objects, whose bearings are taken and then laid off on a chart to plot the ship's position.

Cross head A rudder head fitting to connect the steering gear.

Cross jack Pronounced 'cro'jack'. The mizzen 'course' of a ship, bent to the lower mizzen yard; also the yard itself.

Cross pawl A horizontal timber used when building wooden vessels to hold the frames temporarily in position.

Cross seas Choppy seas coming from a different direction to the wind.

Cross someone's bows Pass close ahead. Get in someone's way by any thwarting action or intention.

Cross trees On large sailing vessels these are the heavy timbers secured athwartships on a mast, to support the 'tops' (see p 165). In sailing boats they are the spreaders for the shrouds, fitted at the hounds.

Crossed cables, cross in the hawse A ship moored, and having no mooring swivel in her two cables, may swing in such a way that one cable will lie across the other, to form a 'cross'.

Crowd on, crowd sail Carry a press of sail to increase speed.

Crowfoot Several small lines radiating from one point, as from the ring or euphroe used with large awnings.

Crown The base of an anchor where the arms meet the shank.

Crown and wall A wall knot formed on a crown knot.

Crown knot A knot made on the end of a rope to start a back splice or to form a larger knot; the ends are unlaid and laid over the rope, then passed over one bight and through the next, thus interlocking them.

Crow's nest A lookout platform or shelter erected high on the foremast.

Cruiser A keel boat designed with living space for the crew (see also **Cabin** and **Day cruiser**, pp 33 and 51). A fast warship fitted with light armament and capable of ranging far from her base.

Cruiser stern A stern built with a fuller form down to and at the waterline, the projecting part being under the water.

Crupper chain That which secures the heel of a jib boom when fitted to a bowsprit, to prevent its rising.

D

Crutch A supporting framework in which to rest a boat. The support used in yachts for stowing the main boom. A portable rowlock to fit in a gunwale, as a fulcrum for an oar shipped in it.

Crutch lanyard A small line spliced to the eye in the inboard end of a crutch, to prevent its loss overboard if accidently unshipped.

Cubby hole Any small space used as a utility store, etc (from **Cuddy**).

Cuddy A small cabin in the fore part of a boat or lighter; in small boats the space below any decked part.

Cunningham hole An eye made in the luff of a sail above a tack cringle, for temporarily altering the set of a sail.

Current The horizontal movement of water; 'setting' is its direction and 'drift' is the rate at which it flows.

Custom of the port Refers to any established rules, customs, or methods that prevail at a certain port.

Cut a feather Create a picturesque bow wave at high speed.

Cut and run A shortened version of 'cut your cables and run for safety', from the days when hempen cables were in use. Any ship or person fleeing from sudden danger may be said to have 'cut and run'.

Cut on the bias A sailmaking term referring to the cutting of the 'gores', ie cloths that gradually widen.

Cut splice A splice used when an eye is required at some place along a rope; it is formed by cutting through where required, and splicing the ends of each rope into the other at a short distance along, to form an eye of the size required.

Cutter A sailing vessel, usually of narrow beam, with one mast, gaff mainsail and staysail, and a jib to a bowsprit. A sloop-rigged ship's boat that pulls double-banked

Cutting Tides are said to be cutting when they are diminishing, ie during the period from springs to neaps.

Cutting a dido Said of a sailing boat caught in confused winds or currents.

Cutwater The fore part, or curved portion, of a ship's stem.

Cyclone A rotary storm in warm latitudes. An area of low barometric pressure.

Daddler The mizzen.

Dagger board The wooden drop keel.

Dagger knees Supporting ties set obliquely between beams and timbers.

Dan buoy A spar having some kind of buoyancy affixed at its centre and one end secured to a weight by a mooring rope. It is used as a marker buoy, being easily recoverable.

Dandy The name given to the sail on the mizzen in a ketch or yawl. A vessel rigged like a yawl, but with a jib-headed mizzen and a loose-footed mainsail.

Dandy rig A sloop-like vessel having a jiggermast aft on which is set a small lugsail. A ketch or yawl.

Dandywink A small winch.

Danforth A type of patent anchor in which the stock passes through its crown.

Davit head The upper outboard end of a davit, from which a boat's falls are suspended.

Davits The metal supports from which boats are suspended, fitted with tackles for hoisting or lowering when they are swung outboard; usually erected in pairs and guyed

in position. Any arm of iron or timber so fitted as to project over ladders, anchors, hatches, etc, and used for hoisting.

Davy Jones' locker The bottom of the sea, common graveyard of everything thrown overboard and of sunken ships.

Day cruiser A cabin cruiser not fitted out for sleeping.

Day's work The record of courses steered, distances made good, etc, kept on a blackboard or in a bridge book, from which the resultant 'dead reckoning' position is computed daily.

Dead ahead, or **astern** Dead in line with the ship.

Dead calm A flat sea, with no sign of wind or moving currents.

Deadeye, dead men's eyes A round flat wooden block with three holes but no sheaves, through which shroud lanyards are rove.

Dead eyes under Sailing heeled well over. Listing heavily.

Dead flat That part of a ship's side of uniform beam along its length, before narrowing to bow and stern.

Dead lift Any heavy lift with no tackles or machinery to assist.

Dead men   Odd yarns or rope ends, etc, left hanging about untidily.

Dead on end   Said of another vessel when her fore-and-aft line coincides with the line of sight of the observer.

Dead reckoning (DR)   A contraction of 'deduced reckoning', being the estimated position of a ship on a chart by calculations as distinct from plotting an observed position.

Dead slow   The minimum speed possible to retain steerage way.

Dead water   The eddy that closes after a ship when she is moving ahead.

Deaden a ship's way   Retard the way of a vessel by luffing up and shaking all sails, or otherwise reducing their effect, as when taking soundings in deep water.

Deadhead   A piece of wood used for any special purpose, eg as a marker, anchor buoy, etc.

Deadlight   An iron shutter for fitting over a scuttle.

Deadrise   The amount of rise of a ship's bottom above the base line, as measured at the full breadth of the turn of the bilge.

Deadwood   A wedge-shaped piece of wood that angles the horn timber (see p 91) to the keel of a yacht.

Deck   A horizontal platform supported by the beams to form both a floor and a covering for the space below it. In old sailing ships they were named the upper, main, middle, lower, and orlop decks respectively; in modern vessels these vary to include several others, usually named by a constructional prefix, such as shelter, half, raised, boat, sun decks, etc.

Deck hand   A person employed as a seaman, working at upper deck duties.

Deck head   The underside of a deck.

Deck light   Any strong glass prism or 'bull's eye' fitted into a deck to permit access of light to a compartment below it. A permanent light fitting on or for any deck.

Deck log   A ship's rough log book, in which is recorded all information about working the ship, and other events, as they occur.

Deck out   Dress ship overall.

Deck pipe   The navel pipe (see p 118).

Deck watch   A small watch used for accurate timing of sights and bearings, and checked with the chronometer.

Decked in A deck built on to a small boat to help keep her dry forward will change her description according to its length; she is then 'decked in', 'quarter-decked' or 'half-decked'.

Deep A navigational channel through, or bounded by, shoal water. A name for those soundings which have no special mark on the lead line, and which are reported as Deep 8, Deep 9, etc (the term 'by the deep' is incorrect, there being no mark on the line).

Deep sea line The line used for deep sea soundings, with a lead of 28lb approx. The first 20 fathoms are marked as for the hand line (see p 84), after which each 10 fathoms has an additional knot, with a single small knot intervening at every 5 fathoms. It has now been mostly superseded by sounding machines.

Demise Transfer a vessel for a period of charter, during which time the owner has no control over her.

Demurrage An allowance for the undue delay or detention of a vessel beyond the 'lay days' (see p 104).

Departure An accurate fix or other position on a chart, from which a course is laid. The distance due east or west, in nautical miles, made good by a ship.

Depression A fall in barometric pressure.

Depth of a boat The vertical distance between gunwale and keel.

Depth of a sail The vertical distance between head and foot of a square sail, and the length of the leech of a fore-and-aft sail.

Depth of the sea Measured from the sea level at LWST to the seabed.

Derelict An abandoned ship.

Derrick A pivoted boom used for lifting weights; it is stayed from a mast, and controlled by guys and a topping lift.

Deviation The compass error due to magnetic action of the iron in a vessel or her cargo; the angle between the compass needle and the magnetic meridian.

Deviation card A 'ready-use' card drawn up by recording the deviation as observed by swinging the ship through all points of the compass.

Devil The outboard plank on the upper deck.

Devil's claw A two-pronged claw hook, attached to the forecastle deck, to place over any link of cable to hold it.

Devil's smiles Those deceptive gleams of sunlight that may appear between dark clouds.

Diagonal-built Built with the side planking at an angle of $45°$, with a second layer set crosswise at right-angles to the first (infrequently the second layer may be fore and aft).

Diamond knot Used when a knot is required somewhere along a rope; the strands come out at the top and the rope is laid up again.

Dickey A small seat.

Difference of latitude (diff lat) The distance between any two places, as measured on a meridian.

Difference of longitude (diff long) The distance between any two places, as measured between their meridians.

Different ships, different long splices An old adage used to refer to any differences between one ship and another. Though one may have done a certain thing in a certain way on one's last ship, it is not done that way on this one.

Dimity Strong muslin for light sails. The flying kites of a ship.

Dinghy A small open rowing boat having no conventional design or type, and made of wood or moulded bonded material, without cabin or ballast. Dinghies vary from 8 to 16ft in length, and are used for rowing, sailing, fishing, and all utility purposes. The increasing popularity of sailing has produced many conventional types for racing purposes (see **Class boats**, p 39).

Dip A freely suspended compass needle, when steadied, will show that the end pointing to the nearest pole is inclined to dip slightly. This 'dip' is usually compensated for by the adjustment of small sliding weights, to bring it horizontal.

Dip, to To lower, eg a signal or salute. To drop. To pass anything down or under any obstruction (see also **At the dip**, p 12).

Dipper The bailing ladle.

Dipping Plunging down into the trough of a wave after riding it.

Dipping a light Sailing away from a light until it eventually 'dips' below the horizon.

Dipping lug cutter A cutter having two lugsails, the largest being set forward. The rig is called 'dipping lug and standing main'.

Dipping lugsail A lugsail that has to be lowered a short way down the mast when going about so that the yard and tack may be passed round the mast and then rehoisted and reset for the new tack.

Dipping the ensign The lowering and rehoisting of an ensign as a salute to a passing ship.

Dipsey　The deep sea lead.

Direction of the wind　The quarter from which it comes is always named in this connection.

Dirty wind　See **Wind shadow**, p 174.

Disembark　Leave a ship, after a voyage.

Disengaging gear　Special types of dropping gear for lowering boats when under way; the principle is to release both falls simultaneously to enable the boat to take the water horizontally.

Dismast　Carry away or otherwise remove a ship's mast(s).

Displacement　The weight of the volume of water displaced by a ship.

Distant signal code　An obsolete system of signalling in which each letter is spelt out by the varied position of flags, balls, and cones.

Distraint　Legal seizure of a ship or her goods in lieu of a debt.

Distress　A state of danger requiring assistance.

Distress signals　Statutory indications for use by any vessel that may require assistance. *By Day*: a gun, or other explosive signal, at 1 minute intervals; continuous soundings with any fog sounding apparatus; the International signal flags NC; the ensign hoisted inverted; or the old distant signal showing a flag over a ball. *At Night*: a gun, as by day; a flame, as produced from burning oil or tar, etc; or any rockets, shells, or fireworks with coloured stars, used singly. It should be kept in mind that small boats, having none of these, may resort to waving a garment attached to an oar, while the 'flag over ball' may be improvised by use of a blanket and fender. (See also **Unwritten law of the sea**, p 170.)

Distressed seaman　Term applied to any seafarer who, through no fault of his own, is in need of means and assistance to return home.

Ditch　A general term for the sea. To 'ditch' anything is to throw it overboard, or otherwise dispose of it.

Ditch crawling　Refers to the activities of a boat owner who prefers to keep to safe inland estuaries and avoids open waters.

Ditty bag　A sailor's small bag containing a housewife, scissors, and mending gear, etc; also called a 'jewing bag'.

Ditty box　A small wooden box in which a sailor keeps his personal treasures, letters, photos, etc, under lock and key.

Dividers　An instrument with two movable points, used in chart work.

55

Dock An artificial enclosure for the berthing and retention of ships for any purposes; it may be wet, dry, or floating.

Dock, to To cut off; to curtail. To confine a ship in a dock. In the case of a wet dock the term applies to securing a ship alongside, within a basin, where she remains afloat; in a dry dock, or graving dock, she is positioned, shored up, and the water pumped out (see also **Floating dock**, p 70).

Docking herself Said of a ship or boat forcing out the ooze to make a bed for herself, or settling on 'the putty' (mud).

Dockyard An establishment provided with docks, slipways, workshops, and warehouses, etc, where vessels are constructed, refitted, or laid up. The word correctly applies to naval yards, the private ones being referred to as shipyards.

Dodger A screen of canvas or other material fitted up as a shelter or protection.

Dog A clip used for closing watertight doors. A fanged iron pin, as used to drive into a log for hauling.

Dog, to To dog a line is to pass it spirally around a rope with and in the lay. To dog strands, when finishing off a splice, is to halve them and seize each part to its neighbouring half.

Dog shores Timbers used to shore a vessel on a launching way, the last supports knocked away preparatory to launching.

Dog vane A small length of bunting attached to the rigging to indicate the direction of wind to the helmsman when sailing.

Dog watches The period from 4 pm to 8 pm is split into two 2 hour watches, called the first and last dog (some call them first and second); this is done to make an odd number of watches daily, thus ensuring that whether a crew works in two, three, or four watches, no man will have the same watch the following day.

Doghouse A raised protective covering abaft the cabin in a small boat, for the steering position and all-round visibility.

Dog's lug The projecting portion of a reefed sail between the earing and reef cringles.

Doldrums Windless zones.

Dolly A metal implement used for clenching rivets, rings, etc.

Dolly shop A marine store on shore (formerly had a doll as signboard).

Dolphin A structure erected in a harbour, used for securing a ship.

Dolphin striker

A spar moored in position so that a ship can be moored to it.

Dolphin striker The perpendicular spar below a bowsprit which provides the downward lead for jib-boom martingales.

Dome The copper centre balancing point of the card in a liquid compass.

Dory A flat bottomed boat that is a double ender, with both sides sloping upward and inward.

Dotting the Is and crossing the Ts Very complicated or very bad steering (revealed by the ship's wake).

Double Alter course; round a certain point or object.

Double banked A pulling boat with two men at each oar has her oars 'double banked', while a boat with two oars pulled on one thwart, ie one on each side, is said to pull double banked if there is more than one pair. In olden days it referred to two tiers of oars, one above the other. To double bank a rope is to have men manning it on both sides.

Double bend The double sheet bend (see **Sheet bend**, p 146).

Double bitt Take an extra turn on the bitts as a precaution.

Double block A pulley block

Double topsail schooner

having two sheaves on the same pin.

Double bottoms The spaces between the inner and outer bottom plating of the hull.

Double bowline Name sometimes applied to the bowline on the bight (see p 26).

Double chine Two chines (see p 38) along each side.

Double ender Any boat that is pointed at both bow and stern.

Double knot Any knot that is enlarged by doubling, ie following the ends round once again; an ordinary (single) wall and crown, diamond, or Matthew Walker, etc, is then prefixed 'double'.

Double luff A purchase having two double blocks, with the standing part of the rope secured to the upper block.

Double tide Two consecutive tides occurring at each flood, through the main current running in from two different directions; it is found only in certain places, where the two high tides consequently prolong the period of high water.

Double topsail schooner A ship with topsails on two separate masts, *not* a ship with two topsails on one mast.

57

Double topsails All topsails were formerly whole sails, but were later divided and bent to two yards.

Double whip A rope led through a single block, then down and through a hook block, and secured to, or near, the upper block.

Doubling The turned edge of a sail to which the boltrope is secured. Any extra strengthening piece or strip sewn on a sail.

Doubling the angle on the bow A navigational calculation applied to a chart by twice taking the bearing of an object on the bow as the ship approaches, one bearing being twice the angle of the other; on a steady course the position is plotted by the distance run between the times the two bearings were taken.

Doubling up Duplicating all ropes securing a vessel.

Doublings That part of a built mast (see p 30) where the top of one and the foot of the one extending above it come together.

Douglas scale The International Sea and Swell Scale, on which the relative indications are read off in figures.

Douse A variant of **Dowse** (see below).

Down at the head By the head (see p 32).

Down below Under cover between decks. Below the upper deck.

Down helm Put the helm down to bring a vessel to the wind.

Down stream In the direction a current will ebb. With the current.

Down wind With the wind. Running. To leeward.

Downhaul Any rope specifically fitted to pull anything down from aloft, such as gantlines, sails, dressing lines, etc.

Dowse Lower, smother, or extinguish quickly. Knock down suddenly.

Drabbler An additional piece of canvas laced to the bonnet of a sail as an expedient to increase its depth.

Drag Where a vessel draws more water aft than she does forward, the difference is called the drag; it varies at different speeds.

Drag, to A vessel will drag when her anchor fails to bite (see p 21).

Drag anchor A drogue when used as a sea anchor.

Drag sheet A sail laced to a weighted spar for use as a drogue.

Drag the anchor Make the anchor

'come home' (see **Coming home**, p 45).

Draught   The depth of water necessary for a vessel to float.

Draught marks   Figures of 6in depth, permanently marked on the stem and sternpost at every foot. Any other markings that may be used for loading or ascertaining the draught of a vessel.

Draw   A sail is said to draw when the wind fills it sufficiently to strain the sheets. A vessel with a certain draught is said to draw that amount of water.

Draw knot   Any knot so formed that when one end is doubled on its bight, it may be quickly and easily pulled undone.

Dress ship   Hoist ensigns at all masts as a sign of respect.

Dress ship overall   Hoist a string of flags from the bow to the masthead, between masts, and down to the stern, in addition to masthead ensigns. Only done on special occasions.

Dressing line   The special line rove to carry the flags aloft when dressing ship overall.

Dressing sails   The treatment of sails by the application of oils, ochre, etc, to render them waterproof and keep away mildew.

Drift   Float along with the tide. A small current caused by the action of the wind. The distance between any two things, such as the blocks of a tackle, the chains and the waterline, etc (see also **Current**, p 50).

Drift anchor   Any kind of drogue when used as a sea anchor for the main purpose of riding to it head to wind.

Drift lead   A hand lead, when dropped on the bottom and left to indicate whether an anchored vessel is starting to drag; the line, made fast inboard, is tended by the 'anchor watch' (see p 10).

Drift sail   A sail, bent to a spar, weighted and bridled, and immersed during a storm, to help lessen the drift of a vessel.

Drifting   Afloat, unsecured, and carried along by wind or tide without use of any motive power.

Drill   Stout cotton cloth or twilled linen, used for white suits and some light sails.

Drive   To drive a ship is to carry too much sail. She is said to be 'driving' when running before a strong wind. The wind will 'drive her' during a gale.

Driver   The spanker, or mizzen.

Drogue   A bucket or canvas bag,

used forward as a sea anchor or over the stern to check a boat's way.

Drop   The depth of a sail as measured on its middle line.

Drop astern   Pass or move a boat nearer towards the stern. To 'fall astern' signifies to be left behind.

Drop down   Sail, row, drift or move a boat down a river, seawards.

Drop keel   A centreplate or centre-board (see p 36) that may be lowered or partly lowered, to help steady a boat.

Dropping gear   Disengaging gear (see p 55).

Drum head   The head of a cap-stan.

Drummer's plait   A simple plait made by passing a loop of rope through each preceding bight; formed for ornamental work.

Dry cleaning   Planing a wood surface clean instead of scrubbing it.

Dry dock   A dock out of which the water can be pumped.

Dry rowing   'Feathering the oars' properly, thus 'pulling dry'. An admonition to 'row dry' or 'pull dry' is made when one dashes spray (with the blade of the oar) into the faces of those sitting in the boat.

Drying features   Any underwater obstructions or markings that will appear, or 'dry out', as the tide recedes.

Dub   Make a plank or other surface smooth and fair.

Duck   An untwilled flaxen material, thicker than calico but thinner than sailcloth, used for light sails and working suits.

Duck, to   To dip. To avoid. To 'duck up' is to move something up-wards and out of the way, eg to trice up a sail to give a helmsman a clear view.

Duffel   Thick woollen cloth, coarsely finished, used to make loose fitting hooded coats for rough wear in cold weather.

Dug-out   A canoe hollowed from a tree trunk.

Dumb barge, dumb lighter   A barge that is not self-propelling and must therefore be towed or warped.

Dumb compass   The pelorus (see p 124).

Dumb fastening   Any temporary screw-hold or other fastening made pending the completion of a proper through fastening.

Dummy   A very strong vertical timber, as fitted in a fishing smack to which the trawl warp is attached.

Dump Throw things overboard.

Dunnage Loose wooden battens, boards, gratings, etc, used to keep cargo clear of water at the bottom of a hold.

Duplex A 'combined lantern' showing a red and green light over the arc of ten points each side of right ahead (red to port).

Dusting A vessel having a rough passage and shipping seas is said to be 'getting a good dusting'.

Dutchman A piece of wood or metal that covers any defective joint.

Dutchman's breeches Patches of blue sky appearing before a gale.

Dutchman's log A piece of timber thrown overboard forward, so that speed may be estimated from the time taken to pass it.

Dutchman's purchase A tackle used in reverse, so that the fall becomes the hoist.

Earing A line used to secure a corner of a sail to a spar. A pendant used to haul down and secure a reef cringle when reefing, or to spread an awning to its stanchion.

Ease off Slacken a rope gradually. Loosen any tight fitting.

Ease the helm Put the helm down a little when close hauled, to meet the sea.

Ease to ten (or other number) A steering order, given when the wheel is too far over, to ease it back until the helm indicator shows that number of degrees—sufficient to keep her turning as required.

Easting The distance gained to the eastward.

Easy An order to reduce any effort applied. Gently, not too fast.

Easy roll A vessel is said to roll 'deep and easy' when her movement is slow and regular without any jerking about.

Eating the wind out of a vessel Obtaining that maximum advantage of wind, trim, and seamanship, whereby a vessel can be made to steal gradually to windward of another.

Ebb The receding tide. Run out. Run low.

Echo sounding The method of sounding whereby electrical impulses from a ship to the bottom are timed on their return; now being developed for other purposes, such as seeking shoals of fish, etc.

61

Eddy A large circular motion of water running contrary to the main stream; when running in the opposite direction to the main stream it is termed a 'back eddy'.

Edge away Sail off the wind from the course steered.

Edge to edge Descriptive of the planking of a carvel-built boat.

Eeking Any additional timber used to make up a required length.

Eight The crew of a rowing boat with eight oarsmen. The boat itself.

Eight bells Struck at the beginning and end of each 4 hour watch, ie at 4, 8, and 12 am and pm (see also **Bell**, p 18).

Elbow, elbow piece A knee (see p 100).

Elbow in the hawse Two crosses in the hawse put in when a ship riding in a tideway swings twice the wrong way, thus causing the two cables to take half a turn on each other.

Embark Go or put on board a ship.

Encased knot An unsound knot in timber surrounded by resin, bark, etc.

End for end Change round a rope by reversing the ends, so that the standing part becomes the hauling part.

End's a-waggin' A phrase used to indicate that the end of any long rope being hauled, reeled, etc, is in sight. Near the end.

English sennet An ornamental plait made with any number of parts each being laid over and under alternately.

Ensign The distinguishing flag used to indicate nationality, flown at or near the stern. It should always be hoisted, and never broken out aloft (see also **Complimentary ensign** p 46).

Ensign staff The long pole erected right aft to carry the ensign.

Entrance The shape of the fore part of a vessel.

Equipment number Used by classification societies to determine the size and number of anchors cables, etc, that a ship requires.

Estimated position The position of a vessel on a chart after allowance have been made for tides, winds, and the courses laid off.

Euphroe A wood or metal fitting from which a number of ropes form a crowfoot for suspending an awning

Even keel, on an Upright. Without a list. Drawing a similar depth of water fore and aft.

Every finger a marline spike Said of a good seaman who is proficient in splicing large wires and other such work.

Every stitch set With all possible canvas set.

Examination vessel Any vessel given the duty of examining others desiring to enter any forbidden area. At night she will carry three red all-round lights vertically 6ft apart, and by day three red balls similarly positioned.

Existence doubtful (ED) A chart notation, eg against a wreck that has been reported but not confirmed.

Expend a mast Carry away or lose a mast in bad weather.

Extra skipper One who has passed for skipper with superior qualifications, and has been granted the highest grade certificate.

Eye The loop of an eye splice.

Eye of an anchor The hole at the top of the shank, to take the ring.

Eye of the wind The direction from which the wind blows.

Eye splice The end of a rope looped back with the strands tucked to form an eye of the size required; if no thimble is used to shape and form a firm splice, it is a soft eye.

Eyebolt A fixed bolt with an open eye in which blocks may be either hooked or shackled.

Eyebrow A rigol (see p 135).

Eyelet holes Small holes in canvas to take a lacing; they may be either sewn in or clenched by brass grommets.

Eyes of her The foremost part of any ship. The hawse holes or pipes.

Eyes of the rigging The soft eyes of the shrouds that fit over a masthead to rest on the hounds.

Facelift A clean-up or fresh coat of paint.

Fag-end An unlaid end of a rope. 'To fag-out' is to unlay an end of rope.

Fair, to make To make anything revert to its proper shape or size; when this is done *in situ*, it is 'made fair in place'.

Fair log The special copy of the deck log written up in ink and signed by the captain; sometimes called a smooth or abstract log.

Fair wind One that enables a boat to be sailed from one place to another without needing to tack or gybe. To 'give a fair wind' is to allow to pass without hindrance.

Fairlead A metal fitting having two guards or arms through which hawsers are led outboard or in any required direction. A bolt, bullseye, or other fitting through which a rope may run.

Fair-water cone The conical cover to a tail shaft, abaft the screw.

Fairway The navigable part of a channel or roadstead.

Fairweather When applied to a person, fitting, boat, or plans made, it means they are likely to prove unreliable in bad weather.

Fake A single ring of a coil of rope.

Fall That part of the rope of any purchase rove between the standing and hauling parts of blocks, frequently including the hauling parts when applied to boats' falls led through a 'leading block' on deck and run out for hoisting.

Fall aboard Come in contact with another vessel broadside on.

Fall astern Drop back. Reduce speed and get astern of another vessel.

Fall away Lose ground. Make excessive leeway.

Fall down Drift downstream with the current.

Fall foul of Entangle with any obstruction.

Fall in with Sight and contact another ship at sea. Meet.

Fall tub A wooden container in which a boat's falls are coiled.

Falling home Tumbling home (see p 168).

Falling off Said of the ship's head when it moves away to leeward of the course.

Falling out Falling without the perpendicular. The flare (see p 68).

False keel An additional keel fitted to the bottom for protection. The wooden end of a yacht's keel for attaching the rudder. The name is often applied to a centreboard or plate also.

False points The three-letter points of the compass.

False stem A fine tapered cutwater affixed to the stem of some yachts.

False tack Luffing as if going

about and then paying off on the same tack (often used to advantage to trick competitors in races).

Fan along   Sail along slowly in very light winds.

Farewell buoy   The last buoy of a channel at the seaward end.

Fash   An irregular seam.

Fashion piece   Timbers secured athwartships aft at the transom.

Fast   A hawser used to secure a vessel, eg headfast, sternfast, etc, often termed headrope, sternrope, etc. Any bollard or projection especially placed in position to take these ropes.

Fathom   A nautical measuring unit equalling 6ft, applied to rope lengths and to depths. A rough approximation is that of the span between both arms horizontally extended.

Fathom, to   To get to the bottom of.

Fathom mark   It is customary in ships to mark off a deck plank with small copper nails 6ft apart, as a handy measure.

Faying   Joining closely together.

Feather, to   To turn the blade of an oar horizontal as it leaves the water at the end of each stroke, and to keep

it thus while reaching aft for the next stroke, thereby lessening its resistance to air, wind, and spray (see also **Dry rowing**, p 60).

Feather-edged   Applied to any plank with one edge thinner than the other.

Featherway   A groove cut for the key of a pin, eg in a shackle.

Feeler   The small metal rod used with sounding machines; it is laid lightly across the wire reeling off the drum to register the slackness as the lead touches bottom.

Felloes, fellows   Wooden pieces making up the rim of a steering wheel.

Fend, fend off   Push a boat clear of any object by means of hands, boathooks, oars, etc.

Fenders   Any specially made buffers of suitable material, suspended by a lanyard; being portable, they are placed where necessary to prevent damage to a ship when berthing or from another vessel coming alongside. They are taken in when getting under way.

Fetch   Sail a distance close hauled without tacking. A boat is said to 'fetch it' when she has reached an objective. It may be said that a boat 'fetches up' at a certain place when missing her objective.

Fetch a compass Go round in a circle.

Fetch the pump Prime it by pouring water into it.

Fibre-glass boat A new type of boat whose hull has been moulded in a bonded compound of fibre-glass material. Being light and strong, they have become popular.

Fid A large conical piece of wood used for opening the strands of large hawsers when splicing. The iron or wooden pin used to keep the heel of a topmast or bowsprit securely in place.

Fiddle Any small wooden frame used at sea to keep plates, etc, from falling off a table.

Fiddle block A double block with one sheave over the other.

Fiddle head An ornamental scroll on the bows in lieu of a figurehead.

Fiferail An iron rail fitted near a mast, a few feet above the deck, carrying belaying pins to which running rigging is secured.

Figure eight knot A knot shaped like an eight, with each part over and under. Easy to make or undo, it is handy for preventing a line un-reeving.

Figurehead Any ornamental figure, head, bust, or similar design fitted under the bowsprit and usually associated with the ship's name.

Fill Fill the sails with wind, eg after being hove to, etc.

Fillings Timber introduced to make good a defective moulding way.

Fine entry, fine entrance A lean bow. A quality possessed by any vessel with long tapered bows to offer less resistance.

Fine lines The qualities of a vessel with a fine entrance, raked masts, narrow beam, and a fine run aft.

Fine on the bow Said of anything bearing within 45° from right ahead.

Fine reach A reach with the wind just before the beam.

Finishings Ornamentations, eg those affixed to a quarter gallery.

First, first watch From 8 pm to midnight, so called because it is the first of the three night watches.

First and last The jocular name applied to the nearest inn to one's moorings, since it is the first call on arrival and the last when leaving.

Fish Strengthen a cracked or broken mast, yard, or spar, etc, by lashing pieces of timber called 'fishes' to it.

Fish an anchor Secure an anchor at the ship's side. The flukes are hoisted by the fish tackle, and the shank painter passes around the shank.

Fish front The rounded timber on the fore side of a made mast.

Fisherman's anchor The oldest type of anchor, with the stock fixed at right-angles to the shank; very useful for small craft.

Fisherman's bend Used for bending a rope to an anchor. It is made by passing two round turns round the ring, and then passing the end within them, finishing off with a half hitch taken on the rope; the end may be stopped back for neatness.

Fisherman's grease Salt water applied for lubrication.

Fisherman's knot Used to bend two small lines together. It is made by forming an overhand knot in the end of each line in such a way that each contains the other line; both knots are then pulled close to each other, forming one knot.

Fisherman's reef Keeping the mainsail set but giving it plenty of sheet.

Fisherman's staysail A large topsail as used in schooners, set above a main staysail.

Fishing boats Vessels of any size that may be engaged in fishing by any methods for catch other than seals, walrus, or whales.

Fishing lights The lights that, in varying circumstances, must be shown, as laid down in the Rule of the Road, by any vessel engaged in fishing.

Fishing lines Lines supplied in hanks for fishing and many other purposes, and named according to size, from 'snooding' to whiting-, mackerel-, cod-, albacore-, dolphin-line, etc.

Fishing smack A sloop-rigged fishing vessel that is fitted out with a well to preserve the catch alive until reaching harbour.

Fit out, fitting out Correctly applies to new vessels when launched and 'taken in hand' for completion, usually in a 'fitting-out' basin; often used to refer to the general overhaul of all gear in preparation for a voyage, racing, a new season, or some other special purpose. Periodical overhauls are properly called 'refits'.

Five-fathom line A contour line of demarcation shown on charts by a continuous dotted line (on older charts it is a series of five dots). It is often taken as a safety line by all but large ships. A measured length of small line marked off as a 'tape measure'.

Fix To take a fix is to ascertain the

67

position of the ship by the intersection of any two or more bearings taken at the same time.

Fixed and flashing Applied to a fixed light becoming momentarily more brilliant at regular intervals.

Fixed light A permanent steady light.

Fizgig, fishgig A metal implement with two or more prongs; it is fitted atop a staff, and, with line attached, is used for spearing fish. Neptune's trident is a fizgig.

Flag The colours of a nation. A rectangular piece of bunting, of any colour(s) or design, used for identification, signalling, etc.

Flag of distress The red ensign, or national flag of any vessel, when hoisted upside down or at half mast (see also **Distress signals**, p 55). Any tattered clothing worn or garments displayed so as to be visible from outboard.

Flagship A ship in which a flag officer sails, or which wears his flag. A person or group who may be leading in any event or race (not necessarily to do with ships).

Flagstaff A mast or pole erected on shore; the term is not applied to anything used on board a ship.

Flake A single ring of rope or coil.

68

Flake, flake down Lay a rope on a deck in flakes, in a flat layer, often ornamental but always ready to run freely.

Flaking a mainsail Stowing a mainsail by lowering it slowly and laying it in bights equally on both sides of the boom.

Flam The flare (see below).

Flank With all possible speed; in excess of normal 'full speed'.

Flap To get into a flap is to get over-excited, trying to do too much at once or in too great a hurry (from the sudden jerky movements of sails in light winds).

Flare The curve of the freeboard from the bows, upward and outward, providing additional rising surface to oncoming waves.

Flashing light A recurring navigational light in which the period of light is shorter than the interval.

Flat Any mud- or sandbank that is practically level across its whole extent and uncovers at low tide.

Flat aback Sails pressed to the mast by the wind are 'flat aback' (see **Aback**, p 7).

Flat aft, flat in Said of any fore-and-aft sail when its sheet is hauled to the full extent.

Flat bottom A boat with no curvature to her bottom.

Flat end The stern, as opposed to the pointed end, the bows.

Flat knot The reef or square knot.

Flat out Said of a power-driven vessel when under way at utmost speed.

Flat seam A seam made by overlapping two edges of canvas and sewing the edge of each to the standing part of the other.

Flat seizing Used for binding two parts of a rope together. An eye is formed in the end of a length of spunyarn, line, or seizing-wire, which is passed round the ropes; the end is rove to make a complete turn, which is hauled taut in the required position; several more taut turns are then passed around both ropes; and the seizing is finished off with a clove hitch round all the turns.

Flat spin A state of bewilderment.

Flat-iron Any vessel of shallow draught, abnormally wide in the beam, and with low upperworks.

Flatten a sail Remove any baggy effect from a sail.

Flatties Small dinghies constructed with flat bottoms.

Fleet A number of ships of any one nation, company, or other group. The amount of work—painting, cleaning, etc—that can be completed from a stage in one position.

Fleet along Spread out along. Move anything a short distance. Shift a stage to the next fleet.

Flemish coil A rope coiled down flat, with each coil lying close within the preceding one and the end coming to the centre.

Flemish eye A soft eye made by unstranding back to a whipping, and then unlaying the yarns, each of which is knotted at a different position around a fid or spar of the size eye required; the formed eye is bound together and the long ends tapered on the standing part, the whole being neatly served over.

Flemish horses The short outer footropes on a yard; those that are outboard of the iron band that takes the slings.

Fleur de lys The decorative north point as printed on compass cards and compass roses (see (p 46).

Flexible steel wire rope Wire rope that is manufactured pliant enough to be brought to a capstan or bollard, etc. When extra flexibility is required, as for reeving through a block, etc, 'extra flexible' steel wire rope is used.

Flinders bar A bar of soft iron mounted vertically on a binnacle to compensate for the induced magnetism of a ship.

Float Be waterborne. A large flat-bottomed boat or platform. Any small light object used as a buoy.

Floated out Built in a dock or enclosed space and floated out by the admission of water.

Floater A life-jacket.

Floating anchor A 'sea anchor' (see p 142).

Floating clause A clause that may be inserted in a charter stating that the vessel shall always lie afloat.

Floating dock A buoyant platform so constructed that it may be flooded and lowered to permit the entry of a ship; after the ship is shored up, the dock is gradually raised by pumping, until both ship and platform are high and dry above water level.

Floating harbour Baulks of timber moored in a position ahead of a ship to break the force of the sea.

Floating light A light affixed to a buoy or other object afloat, as distinct from one on shore. Describes a vessel showing low draught marks, or appearing to be on and not in the water.

Flogging Working excessively.

Flood The flood tide is the rising or incoming tide. High water.

Flood, to To open a seacock or other inlet, or otherwise fill a compartment with water, by accident or for any specific purpose.

Floorboards Wooden battens or gratings shaped to cover the floors of boats and to make a walking surface. Bottom boards.

Floors The bottom transverse vertical supporting timbers on which the bottom of a ship is framed and bolted to the keel.

Flotsam Goods lost by shipwreck, or anything that has gone overboard and is later found floating at sea.

Flower of the winds Obsolete term for the fleur de lys (see p 69).

Flowing sheet A sheet that is eased well off and controlling a well filled sail when running.

Fluke The pointed triangular end of the arm of an anchor. A light air of variable strength and duration sometimes called 'fluky'.

Flurry A sudden gust of wind or rain that passes on.

Flush Level, or in line with.

Flush deck An upper deck flush from bow to stern, or over its full length, with no superstructures or side-to-side erections on it.

Fly The lengthwise expanse of a flag, but, more generally, the lower corner farthest from the mast, where-on a device may be worn. A strip of bunting affixed to a shroud for use as a wind indicator.

Fly to Come quickly up into the wind.

Fly-by-night A jib sometimes used by sloops when running.

Flying bridge A light fore-and-aft bridge above the upper deck.

Flying gybe The careless action of gybing without first trimming the sail amidships, thus permitting the boom to swing over a wide arc quickly and very often dangerously.

Flying jib-boom A small boom fitted out and beyond the jib-boom, to take the flying jib.

Flying kites Additional upper sails used in fine weather.

Flying light Applied to a ship under way with draught marks well out of the water or showing much less than her normal draught; also of anyone who has no belongings to hand other than the clothes he wears.

Flying-fish sailor One who selects his ships for their voyages through the tropics, and avoids sailing through colder climes.

Foam The whitish froth appearing when salt water is agitated.

Fog Reduced visibility brought about by particles of moisture that form clouds in the air; sailors usually consider it foggy when the visibility drops to less than a mile.

Fog bell Term applied to any bell used by vessels at anchor, by light-houses, or at the end of jetties, etc, during fog; also used to describe the bell affixed to any moored buoy (bell buoy).

Fog buoy A buoy or inflated bag towed well astern during fog to assist any vessel in company to follow in comparative safety by keeping it sighted. Any buoy fitted with a fog bell.

Fog horn The apparatus used by sailing ships, shore stations, etc, during a fog. A ship's siren when used as such.

Fog lookouts Men placed right forward, aft, and also well aloft during fog to augment the normal lookouts.

Fog signals Sound signals pro-duced by vessels under way during fog, as prescribed by the Rule of the Road. A steam vessel having way on her shall sound one prolonged blast every 2 minutes; if under way, but stopped and having no way on her, she shall sound two consecutive blasts every 2 minutes. A sailing vessel shall sound at 1 minute intervals, one blast if on the starboard tack, two blasts if on the port tack, and three blasts if the wind is abaft the beam. Any vessel towing or unable to manoeuvre, not being under control, shall sound three blasts in succession, one prolonged followed by two short blasts. Vessels at anchor ring a bell rapidly for 5 seconds every minute.

Fogbound Unable to proceed because of fog.

Folded up Said of anything that has carried away or collapsed.

Folding stock The stock of an anchor so made that it can be folded back along the shank when not in use.

Folding tiller A tiller in two lengths, bolted together, which may be extended for use as one piece or folded back double out of the way.

Following sea The sea running with the ship.

Following wind A wind coming from behind a ship.

Foot The lower edge of a sail or any other fitting or article.

Foot down Tauten a rope by standing on it to make a bight; thus the slack may be taken in.

Footrope The rope to which the lower edge of a sail is secured. The rope slung under a yard or bowsprit, etc, for use of seamen when furling sails.

Forbes log An electric recording device that carries a rotating vane protruding through the bottom of a vessel.

Fore In, towards, or of the foremost part of any vessel. A prefix applied to that one of many which is nearest the bows.

Fore and aft Lengthwise of a ship; in line from bow to stern.

Fore course The sail bent to the fore lower yard.

Fore gripe The piece of wood clenched to the keel which takes the stempiece.

Fore guy Any rope that leads forward from a boom, davit, derrick, etc, to place and keep it in position.

Fore hook The breast hook (see p 28).

Fore horse An iron bar fitted athwartships on the foredeck for the fore sheet to travel on.

Fore peak The small part of a ship's hold right forward. The small space in the bows of boats that are decked in.

Fore sheets The rope or tackle used to control the set of the foresail.

Fore stay A wire rope fitted from the masthead to the bowsprit end (or to the stem of boats having no bowsprit), supporting the mast.

Fore top A platform erected at the foremasthead (see **Top**, p 165).

Fore-and-aft-rigged A sailing vessel without square sails but with all her canvas set in her fore-and-aft line.

Fore-and-after A fore-and-aft rigged vessel. The tackle and pennant between the two blocks of any patent dropping gear, which, when set up, enable the pins to be removed, and when released, will permit the boat to disengage and drop clear. Any special purpose rope that may run in a fore-and-aft direction.

Forecastle (abbrevs, **Fo'c'sle, Fxle, Fx,** pronounced 'folksle') Formerly the cabin or castle before the foremast, but now generally used for that part of the foredeck, or its superstructure, containing the anchors and cables or the crew space below it; differentiated by 'on the fo'c'sle' for working cables, etc, and 'in the fo'c'sle' for crew space.

Foredeck That part of the deck before the bridge or foremast.

Forefoot That point where the stem joins the keel.

Forelock A flat splayed pin that fits in the end of a shackle pin, stock, etc, to prevent its withdrawal.

Foremast The forward mast of any ship having two or more masts.

Foremost An object so identified is that one nearest the bows.

Forenoon watch The watch kept from 8 am to noon (for lunchtime convenience it is often extended to 12.30 pm).

Forereach Shoot ahead in stays. Headway that is gained after turning into the wind, before stopping and gathering sternway. Lie close to the wind with intent to make little way and avoid stopping 'in irons'—by keeping a minimum of wind and gradually creeping ahead instead of sailing close hauled.

Foresail The lowest square sail on the foremast of a ship, barque, or brig; in a schooner it is a gaff fore-and-aft sail and sets abaft the mast, while in a cutter or sloop it is jib-shaped; and in small boats with only two sails it is the foremost one. When triangular and hanked to a forestay, it is called a forestaysail.

73

Foreshore That part of any shore between high and low water mark.

Forespring Opposite to backspring (see p 14).

Foretopmast The mast next above the foremast (above that again is the foretopgallantmast).

Formula boats Racing boats constructed to comply with a variable formula that covers waterline length and sail area, etc.

Forward, forrard The fore part of a ship. At or near the bows.

Fothering Temporarily closing a leak by means of a sail filled with oakum and passed under the boat into position.

Foul Describes anything that will not run clear, becomes entangled, forms an obstruction, collides, or prevents free passage.

Foul anchor Term used when the cable or some other obstruction is round the flukes of an anchor.

Foul berth One occupied by any vessel that anchors without having sufficient swinging space to enable her to keep clear of other vessels, or of any obstructions or objects in her vicinity.

Foul bottom A hull covered with

weed, barnacles, or other marine growth.

Foul ground An anchorage where the bottom is littered with wrecks or other obstructions, which may cause a foul anchor.

Foul hawse Turns put into cables by a ship swinging round and causing them to cross or putting a turn or turns in them.

Foul wind One that blows from the direction a ship requires to make, or one that may set a ship in danger.

Found Equipped or maintained; a vessel is said to be 'well found' when she is well fitted out.

Founder Go to the bottom. Fill with water and sink.

Four-point bearing A method used on a steady course to fix the ship's position. It refers to four points of the compass and not four objects, only one such being required. A bearing of the object is taken twice, eg when abeam and when on the bow (45°), or any other four points difference, and the time is noted in each case; the 'distance run' in the interval will enable the course to be correctly plotted on the chart, and show the position.

Four-poster Any sailing vesles with four masts.

74

Fox a nettle Twist or plait a yarn for points and grafts.

Foxey Describes any timber when discoloured as a sign of decay.

Foy A small narrow boat, with oars and a lugsail for occasional use; commonly used in some places to assist ships when securing.

Frame The skeleton of a vessel. A transverse structure between ribs.

Framing The structure of ribs, frames, etc, to which a ship's outside plating is affixed.

Franchise A certain fixed percentage of the insured value of a vessel that cannot be claimed when loss is incurred.

Frap Bind anything taut in place by passing a rope around it.

Frapping line A rope used to frap anything, especially awnings during inclement weather, ie to prevent excessive flapping movement.

Free A wind is said to free a ship sailing close hauled when it moves farther abeam (see also **Running free** and **Sailing free**, pp 139 and 140).

Free alongside ship A term meaning that no responsibility is incurred until goods are actually alongside the ship.

Free on board (FOB) Goods to be delivered on board without charge.

Free puff Sailing term for a favourable gust needing weather helm.

Freeboard The side of a ship above water level to the upper deck, or the height of the same.

Freeing port An opening in the bulwarks for the freeing of any water that has been shipped.

French bowline Made somewhat similarly to a bowline, except that two bights are made instead of one; frequently used as an alternative to a bowline on the bight.

Frenchman A left-hand loop or turn put in if needed to counteract twists when coiling down right-handed rope.

Fresh hand at the bellows Said when a gale suddenly freshens.

Freshen A wind is said to freshen when it increases in strength.

Freshen hawse Pay out a short length of cable (when rope cable is used) to relieve the chafe.

Freshen the nip Veer or haul slightly so that a rope may be moved a little, in order to replace any part subject to chafing.

75

From stem to stern From one end to the other.

From truck to keel From top to bottom.

Frostbiter One who takes part in sailing races held in winter or cold weather, or goes sailing for pleasure despite frost or snow.

Full and by Sailing with the sails full and as close by the wind as is

possible without lifting or shaking the sails.

Full and change The time of new or full moon, when the high water occurs at a fixed time.

Full due To secure anything 'for a full due' is to do so when it is unlikely to be used again for some time.

Full for stays An order given a helmsman to keep the sails full of wind for going about so that she may round easily.

FOREMAST		MAINMAST		MIZZENMAST	
1	Foresail (or course)	1	Mainsail (or course)	1	Crossjack (furled)
2	Lower fore topsail	2	Lower main topsail	2	Lower mizzen topsail
3	Upper fore topsail	3	Upper main topsail	3	Upper mizzen topsail
4	Lower foretopgallant sail	4	Lower maintopgallant sail	4	Mizzen topgallant sail
5	Upper foretopgallant sail	5	Upper maintopgallant sail	5	Mizzen royal
6	Fore royal	6	Main royal	6	Spanker or driver
		7	Main skysail		

STAYSAILS		JIBS		
1	Main topmast staysail	1	Flying jib	(Yards and rigging
2	Main topgallant staysail	2	Outer jib	have been omitted
3	Royal staysail	3	Inner jib	for clarity)
4	Mizzen topmast staysail	4	Jib	
5	Mizzen topgallant staysail			

Full-rigged ship's sails

Full-rigged ship A ship with three or more masts and with all square sails set on all masts.

Furl Roll, fold, gather, or make up any sail, awning, canvas, etc.

Furniture The fittings essential to any vessel, comprising her masts, boats and davits, capstan, etc.

Furrens, fillings Pieces that are used to double or extend the timbers.

Furrow To 'cut a furrow' is to create a bow wave (see p 26).

Futtock plate The metal plate at the edge of a lower top, fitted to take the dead eyes of topmast rigging.

Futtock shrouds, futtock rigging Rope or chain securing the futtock plate to a band on the mast below it.

Futtocks The separate built-up pieces forming a wooden ship's timbers.

Gaff The spar to which the head of a fore-and-aft mainsail is bent. A spar angled to a mast, on which flags are hoisted at the peak. A metal hook on a handle, eg for lifting fish inboard.

Gaff topsail A triangular sail with the head extended on a gaff, which is set from or hoisted on a topmast; it is clewed out to the peak of the main gaff.

Gaff-headed, gaff sail Any sail with which a gaff is used.

Gale A strong wind between a stiff breeze and a hurricane.

Galled Worn or scored as a result of friction caused by chafing, to prevent which all places exposed to it should be covered with ropes, mats, pads, canvas, etc.

Galley The cookhouse.

Gallows A U-shaped iron supporting arch, as fitted on trawlers to carry the block for working the trawl. A frame to support a boom.

Gallows bitts A frame erected on deck for supporting spare booms, spars, oars, etc.

Gamming Exchanging conversation with someone on another vessel (from the term once used when crews on two vessels in close proximity would stop and speak to each other when away from home for long periods).

Gammon iron The iron hoop fitting on a stem head to take a bowsprit.

Gammonings Lashings that secure a bowsprit in place.

Gangplank A long narrow plank, fitted with treads, to enable people to walk over the bow of a beached

77

boat; it is stowed fore and aft amidships on the thwarts when not in use.

Gangway A passage or way by which to enter or leave a vessel. To 'make a gangway' is to clear a walking space.

Gangway ladder A ladder over the side from a gangway to boat level.

Gantline A rope through a block fixed aloft, and used for hoisting sails or other articles, or as a clothes line, etc.

Garboard, garboard strake The whole length of planking on each side, next to the keel.

Garnet A small tackle fitted on a stay for a clew line.

Gaskets Rope or canvas securing bands. Tiers (see p 164).

Gather way Feel the impulse of the wind on the sails, or, in power boats, begin to move through the water and obtain steerage way.

Gear A general comprehensive term for equipment, usually prefixed by the particular articles referred to, eg sailing gear, cleaning gear, etc.

General drill The exercising of a crew in various activities, such as preparing to tow or be towed, laying out a kedge, etc.

General routine The normal daily round and common tasks.

Genoa A large jib for racing; more like a spinnaker than a headsail.

German eye splice A variant of the normal eye splice, having the first strand tucked with the lay and not against it.

Get the steam roller out Expresses the wish that the sea may calm down.

Get to windward Gain an advantage over.

Ghosting Under sail and making way when there seems to be no wind.

Gig A long light boat with two masts, lateen-rigged, and single banked for pulling; it is sometimes called a galley.

Gig stroke, galley stroke A smart ceremonial method of rowing, each stroke being longer than normal; at the end of each stroke the crew remain lying back below the gunwale and pause before reaching aft for the next one, all moving as one.

Gimbals, gymbals A double concentric metal suspension fitting in which a compass bowl, primus stove, etc, may be retained in a horizontal position because it counteracts the motion of the ship.

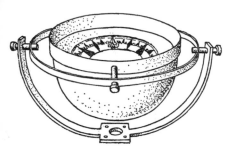

Compass suspended in gimbals

Gin block A large single-sheave all-metal block with a skeleton frame, suspended by a swivel hook.

Ginger string Spunyarn.

Gingerbread Artistic decorative designs carved or moulded on a ship's stern, often covered by gold leaf (hence to 'gild the gingerbread').

Girls have hold of the towrope, the Used when a ship homeward bound is making good speed.

Girt Moored taut by cables to two anchors laid well apart, so that she cannot swing freely to wind or tide and cause one cable to ride along the ship's side. One cable should be veered to permit it to sink clear.

Girtline A gantline (see above).

Give Yield, as a new rope does to strain, or as a seizing surges. Show signs of parting or carrying away.

Give way The command given to a boat's crew to start pulling. A duty, imposed by the Rule of the Road, to take action to prevent collision, and to keep clear of another vessel.

Give-way vessel A vessel whose duty it is to keep clear of another by taking necessary action.

Glass The barometer, the telescope, or the sand glass.

Glim A light of any sort.

Glory hole The fore peak, or any odd corner where anything may be dumped out of the way.

Go aboard Enter or go on to a ship.

Go about Tack. Put the ship's head through the wind; change from one tack to the other.

Go ahead Proceed. Make way, bows first. Start.

Go aloft Climb the ratlines, rigging, or mast. Ascend.

Go ashore Disembark.

Go large Sail with the wind near the quarter.

Go off the deep end Rant and roar.

79

Go to leeward A phrase signifying a loss or disadvantage in any way.

Goalposter A vessel with a large horizontal high girder athwart the upper deck, for use with gantries, derricks, etc.

Going home Said of any article when practically worn out.

Gone by the board Said of a mast that breaks off at deck level. Disappeared overboard. Lost.

Good board To sail on a straight line of a course, without falling to leeward, when on a wind is to make a good board or gain.

Goose neck A jointed hinged fitting by which the heel of a boom is kept to the mast but permitted to turn in any direction.

Goose-wing Sail with mainsail set one side and foresail set the other side, so that one will not blanket the other.

Gorge The groove in the sheave of a block to take the rope.

Goring That part of the skirts of a sail (cut on the bias), where it gradually widens; each cloth so cut is a gore.

Got her cable Said of a ship as her anchor bites and she 'rides' to it.

Grablines Name often given to the

lifelines suspended outboard in bights on each side of a lifeboat from gunwale to waterline.

Graft Ornamental weaving of the yarns to cover a splice.

Granny knot A 'false' reef knot with the second tie crossed the wrong way, insecure under strain and difficult to untie if jammed.

Grapnel A small anchor with two or more flukes. It is not intended for holding when great strength is required, but for use mainly as a grappling iron. The rope or chain used as cable in a boat.

Grappling iron A small grapnel used for the recovery of articles from the bottom (from irons formerly used to secure to enemy ships).

Grass, grass line A very rough line or rope made from coconut fibres. Very light, resilient, and buoyant, it is weaker than other ropes. It is also known as 'coir' or 'bass'.

Grating A framework of bars. Bottom boards, covers, etc, sometimes ornamented with wooden lattice-work.

Graving Cleaning a ship's bottom and coating it with some protective (hence the term 'graving dock' where this may be done).

Grease the ways Prepare for

launching. Applied to any advance preparations.

Great Bear, the The constellation containing 'the Pointers' (see p 126).

Greenhorn, green hand A gullible novice uninitiated into nautical life. 'Acting green' is feigning or displaying apparent ignorance.

Gridiron A wood or metal staging positioned to receive a vessel and contain her for examination during the falling tide.

Gripe The cutwater. The curved timber joining the stem to the keel.

Gripe, to A boat is said 'to gripe' if she is carrying too much weather helm. To 'gripe' a boat is to bowse it to a griping spar or in its crutches, to prevent movement at sea.

Gripes Long bands of matting or canvas fixed to each davit head and passed round a boat to secure it in position; they are crossed outboard and secured to a slip for instant release.

Griping spar A long spar with pudding fenders, shipped between davits, to which a boat is griped and from which the 'scrambling net' is hung.

Grocer's hitch Name applied to any kind of nondescript hitch that slips, jams, or is a nuisance to replace.

Grog Rum diluted with water as a check against intoxication.

Grommet A rope ring made from a single strand laid round three times. A small brass eyelet hole fitted into sails, canvas screens, etc, for passing lacings.

Ground Take the ground or bottom, or touch the shore, either intentionally or by accident. 'Grounding' is the act of deliberately laying a ship ashore for any purpose.

Ground scope The length of cable which remains under water between two anchors or 'clumps' used as moorings for small boats.

Ground sea A succession of rollers that roll in to break on a shore in calm weather. At sea it is called a 'ground swell'.

Ground tackle Collective term for anchors, cables, etc, used for laying out as moorings. Gear used for hauling off when aground.

Ground ways The fixed ways of a building slip over which the sliding ways will run when a launching takes place.

Growing The direction of the cable from the bow. An extended

Groyne, groin A projection of masonry or wood built on a shore to control the drift of shingle or sand.

Guard rail critic One who offers advice or unwanted instructions from inboard to anyone outboard or in a boat.

Guard rails Safety rails fitted round open decks, dock sides, etc; they may be fixed, or comprise stanchions holding wire or chain lengths. They must always be replaced after any temporary removal.

Guard ship The duty ship of naval or other vessels in a port; her boat, used for patrols, etc, is called the 'guard boat'.

Gudgeon An eyebolt affixed to a sternpost, which receives the pintle of a rudder when it is shipped. The rudder eyebolt.

Guest warp A rope led from a boom, or a point forward, to a gangway, for the use of visiting boats or for hauling ahead clear of the side.

Gully A channel or gutter planned for water to run away.

Gun tackle A tackle so named from its use horizontally for hauling and not hoisting (see **Tackles**, p 163).

arm is often used to illustrate a verbal report.

Gunter A sail bent to a gaff and slung from a strop about two-thirds along, the head or gaff being hoisted almost perpendicular. Though four-sided, the throat is so obtuse that, with the luff to the mast, it appears almost a triangular sail.

Gunwales, gunnels The strengthening piece at the top of the hull, fitted all round a boat, which holds the timbers and top strakes (so called because guns were pointed from the wale or upper edge).

Gunwales under With the water lapping over the lee gunwale. Heeled over to the wash strakes while sailing.

Gusset A piece of canvas let in to increase width or strengthen.

Guy A steadying rope used to position a swinging derrick, boom, davit, etc; if more than one, they are differentiated by the direction of their lead, eg fore guy, after guy, etc.

Gybe Turn a sailing boat when the wind is aft, so that the wind passes from one quarter to the other; the opposite to 'staying'. The term is now popularly used, when the wind is on or abaft the quarter, in describing the boat as being 'on the starboard (or port) gybe' instead of 'tack'.

Gybe all standing The sudden swinging over of the mainsail boom when the wind is well aft, caused by getting 'by the lee' (see p 32).

Gybe-O The helmsman's call warning the crew to prepare to gybe.

Gymbals See **Gimbals**, p 78

Gypsy A small drum attached to a winch. Sometimes applied to the sprocket wheel of a windlass that receives the cable links.

Gyro, gyro compass An electrically driven rotating gyroscope aligned with the earth's axis so that it will indicate the true north. The instrument is placed well down within a vessel, and needs expert supervision. It is referred to as the 'master gyro' when there are several repeaters around the vessel.

Gyro repeater A compass card dial, contained in a circular holder, which may be lined up and kept in step with, and by, the master gyro; several may be used thus and positioned where required, eg at the wheel, compass platform, cabin, etc.

Hail Call to any other vessel or boat. A vessel is said to 'hail' from her port of registry and a seaman from his birthplace.

Half cardinals The four inter-cardinal points—NE, NW, SE, and SW.

Half deck A small deck abaft the mainmast to the after superstructure.

Half hitch Pass the end of a rope round its standing part and then bring it up through the bight, forming a simple loop.

Half mast A flag is lowered to half mast as a sign of mourning. The term is also applied to anything not hoisted right up, eg trousers.

Half seas over Walking unsteadily; half drunk.

Half tide The mean level of the sea, during springs or neaps; it is therefore a constant factor.

Half-decker A boat with a deck fitted from forward to half its length.

Halyards, halliards Ropes used for hoisting and lowering flags, sails, yards, etc.

Hambone A sextant.

Hambro, hambroline A small line made of three strands of hemp, hard laid, sometimes tarred, and used for lacings, seizings, etc.

Hammock A swinging bed made of No 0 canvas, 6ft by 4ft, secured at each end by clews, and slung up to supports when in use.

Hand A term for one of a crew; sometimes prefixed by a designation, eg deck hand, cabin hand, galley hand, etc.

Hand, to   To furl. To work at or with.

Hand lead and line   A 10–14lb leg-of-mutton-shaped lead attached to a 20 fathom line is used in all vessels for taking soundings by hand.

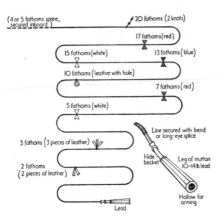

Hand lead and line, with markings
NB. Marks used for feeling in darkness: red (bunting), white (canvas or duck), and blue (serge)

Hand line   A term applied to any line used by hand, such as for sounding, fishing, marking off, etc.

Hand mast   A light pole mast.

Hand over hand   Haul or take up on a rope by passing the hands one over the other to keep it moving continuously. A sailor climbs a rope 'hand over hand' if he does so without using his legs.

84

Hand rail   A rail in lieu of a man-rope as a handhold to a ladder.

Hand reef and steer   The set qualifications once required of a seaman.

Hand taut   Hauled as tautly as possible by hand.

Handicap   An individual advantage in time or distance applied to a boat, according to her rig and design, for racing purposes (see also **Portsmouth yardstick**, p 128).

Handle   To handle a boat or vessel is to sail, con, or control her. A boat may also be said to 'handle well' or otherwise.

Handsomely   Gradually, slowly, with care (when working a rope).

Handspike   A hand lever made of wood, usually shod with an iron heel.

Handy billy   A light watch tackle, fitted with 2in rope or under, especially useful for odd jobs about the upper deck.

Hang out the washing   Hoist and set the sails.

Hanging Judas   A rope or line hanging loose; anything suspended untidily.

Hanging up   Describes a boat alongside a jetty, etc, with securing ropes taut and left hanging by them as the tide recedes.

Hangman's noose A knife lanyard worn round the neck, if made with the knot formed to run instead of being tucked.

Hank A metal clip-ring fitting for bending on staysails. A skein of yarn or small line.

Hank for hank Said of two sailing boats on a wind as they tack together.

Hanked Describes a sail secured by hanks to a stay.

Harbour A natural or artificial area of water partially enclosed.

Harbour dues Charges imposed for use of a harbour.

Harbour master One appointed to supervise the working of a port.

Harbour reach That part of any river that leads into a harbour.

Hard A firm part of a foreshore (or the road leading to it), where heavy articles could be taken down for shipping in boats (from places where guns were run down).

Hard alee An alternative for lee-o (see p 105).

Hard aport or **astarboard** An order to put the helm hard over in the direction indicated. When sailing, the terms 'hard aweather' or 'hard alee' are used instead.

Hard chine A feature of a boat in which the topsides and bottom meet at an angle instead of curving to a round bilge.

Hard down An order to put the helm as far over to leeward as possible.

Hard eye An eye splice containing a thimble.

Hard over An order to put the helm right over farther than it is.

Hard tack Ship's biscuits.

Hard up An order to put the helm as far over to windward as possible.

Harpings Additional planking fitted on the sides at the bows.

Hartford shackle A patent shackle for use when securing to a buoy.

Hatch An opening in the deck for access to the interior of a ship.

Hatch covers Wooden battens, tarpaulins, canvas covers, etc, used to close or cover any hatch or other openings through a deck.

85

Hatch roller A length of pipe-shaped roller fitted on to coamings to prevent chafing of the hoisting whips.

Hatchway An opening in the deck with a ladder to lead below.

Haul Pull on a rope. 'Haul away' is the order to pull.

Haul aft or **forward** Refers to the wind when it changes direction to affect a sailing boat; it 'hauls round' when it veers.

Haul aft a sheet Pull on the rope attached to the clew, to shorten the sheet and bring the clew of the sail farther aft.

Haul her wind A ship is said to haul her wind when she is brought nearer to the wind after running free; a similar action is implied in the terms 'haul to the wind' or 'haul your wind'.

Haul off Alter course away from an object. Pull away, eg a ship from a jetty, etc.

Haul one's wind Change tactics suddenly to dodge something.

Haul out Pull a vessel out from a dock, or haul a boat from the water on to a hard or slipway, etc.

Haul taut Take up the slack of a rope. To 'haul taut singly' applies

to boat's falls, which are hauled taut separately before being married to hoist a boat horizontally.

Have a dekko Take a look at or view something.

Have the heels of another Sail faster than another vessel.

Haven An inlet along a coastline where ships may shelter or anchor.

Hawse That part of a ship where the hawse holes are cut at the bows; correctly it refers to the area through which a cable lies, from ship to anchor, or, when two anchors are laid out, the whole area between both hawse holes and both anchors.

Hawse bag A jackass (see p 96).

Hawse holes Large apertures cut in the bows to take the hawse pipes.

Hawse pipes The protective iron casting fitted to hawse holes, through which the cables run and into which the anchor is secured.

Hawser A stout rope of hemp or wire used for securing alongside, towing, warping, etc; usually applied to ropes of 4½in and over.

Hawser bend A method of joining two hawsers together, quick and easy to make and unlikely to jam; an overhand knot in each end is made to bight them together, and both ends are seized back.

Hawser eye A thimble eye in the end of a hawser. Sometimes a becket of smaller rope tailed and served, to enable it to reeve.

Hawser-laid Describes the normal rope or hawser, as distinct from cable-laid, etc.

Hawsing Yawing and tautening cable when at anchor.

Hazard Expose a vessel to a risk or danger. Take a chance.

Head The bow of a ship. The top side of a square sail; the upper part of a triangular sail. The upper end of any spar, derrick, etc. A shaped vertical timber.

Head and tail Describes similar articles stowed side by side when each is laid the opposite way to its neighbour.

Head on Bows on (see p 26).

Head reaching Forereaching (see p 73).

Head sea One whose waves approach from the direction steered.

Headfast, headrope The securing rope from the bows.

Headroom The clearance between decks.

Heads A ship's latrines.

Headsails All sails that are set before the foremast.

Headstay The stay from the top of a mast of a sailing boat to the bow; the one before any others.

Headway A vessel is said to 'gather headway' when she advances, bows first, and begins to make way through the water.

Heart The centre core around which the strands of a rope are laid up; it is an inferior strand but helps keep them in position.

Heart thimble A thimble thus shaped, as distinct from a round one.

Heave A command to lift or pull together. Throw, cast, or draw.

Heave ahead Haul a ship ahead by warp.

Heave and set The motion of a vessel rising and falling to the waves.

Heave in Start pulling on a rope or 'back up' a rope brought to a capstan, etc, as it starts turning. Shorten in (see p 148).

Heave in sight Come into view from the horizon.

87

Heave short 'Shorten in' the cable until almost over the anchor.

Heave taut Start a capstan, winch, etc, to take up the slack of a cable, or rope brought to, and put the initial strain on it.

Heave the lead Take soundings by the hand lead and line while under way; the lead is swung, jerked round over the head, and released to be cast some distance ahead. A good leadsman will recover the slack, feel the bottom, and note the depth at the waterline when the line is vertical.

Heave to Stop. Trim the sails, or work the engines, so as to keep the vessel almost stationary. Used in the event of emergency or impending danger, as distinct from 'laying to' with intent to stop and wait.

Heave-ho An exclamation for an extra effort to be made together.

Heaving down The heeling or listing of a ship by the use of tackles affixed between masthead and shore, when careening (see p 34).

Heaving line A length of line used as a messenger across a distance; it is coiled in the hand and thrown, eg from a ship to a person outboard, usually so that a stronger line may be bent on and then hauled across. Securing of the inboard end should not be overlooked, nor the line

overweighted so that it becomes a dangerous missile.

Heel The lower end of any mast, boom, spar, or derrick, etc. The point where the sternpost joins the keel.

Heel, to To list under sail.

Heel brace The iron support at the bottom of a rudder.

Heeler A light fast sailing boat with a good performance; she is said to possess a good, or clean, pair of heels.

Heeling error A source of compass error that may occur, especially in boats with deep iron keels, when sailing heeled over.

Helm The steering apparatus controlling the rudder, ie wheel or tiller; with wheel steering, the wheel, rudder, and ship's head all move together to the side ordered, but in boats with no wheel the helm is the tiller, which moves in the opposite direction to the rudder and ship's head.

Helm amidships The rudder in the fore-and-aft line of a ship.

Helm indicator An instrument with a pointer (geared to the wheel), by which the angle of rudder used may be noted at any time.

Helm orders Terms used to con a ship, and passed to the helmsman.

Helm port The space where a rudder passes through a ship's hull.

Helm's alee A helmsman's warning call as he puts the helm down to go about.

Helmsman The man at the wheel or tiller.

Hemp Cordage made from the material of the hemp plant; it may come as white or tarred hemp.

Hermaphrodite Half brig, half schooner. A brigantine.

Herring boning A method used in repairing sails, consisting of a pattern of cross stitches that keep the seams flat.

High and dry Grounded when the tide recedes. Wholly above water level.

High enough An order to stop hoisting.

High tide The greatest elevation of a tide at a certain place.

High water The full of the flood. The time at which a high tide occurs. A mark on shore to which a flood tide reaches is called a 'high-water mark'.

High water, full and change The time interval between the transit of the moon and high water on the days of full and change of the moon; it differs at each port.

Hitch Class of knot used at sea, in which certain parts jam each other when in use and yet are easily unhitched.

Hitch, to To make fast a rope to another or to any object.

Hitch up Join one thing to another. Wed.

Hog The long fore-and-aft frame timber secured over the keel for anchoring the garboards and timbers. It is covered by the keelson, the whole being bolted throughout to resist vertical flexure.

Hogged Refers to a vessel that is higher in the middle through a droop at the ends.

Hogged sheer A sheer line highly curved amidships; opposite to a 'bold sheer' (see p 25).

Hogging The tendency of any boat improperly crutched, or cradled only in the middle, to develop a droop at her ends. Cleaning the ship's bottom with stiff brushes called 'hogs'.

Hogging line For use with a collision mat, or hogging the bottom (see **Bottom line**, p 26).

89

Hoist Raise, lift, or haul up. A method used to lift. The contents of a sling at each hoist or lift. The height of a sail. A string of signal flags.

Hoist the flag The term is often used before a sailing race, when the flag is hoisted at the firing of the 10 minute warning gun, when the preparative goes up 5 minutes before the start, or for any other special occasions or meanings (see **Colours**, p 45).

Hold A special compartment or interior space used for stowing cargo.

Hold on to the land Keep near though not always in sight of land.

Hold on to the slack Be idle.

Hold water A command used in rowing boats to dip the blades vertically into the water and keep them there to check the way.

Holding ground The nature of the bottom and its holding quality for purposes of anchoring.

Holidays Bare patches missed when painting, cleaning, etc.

Hollow run A ship's lower counter when arched below the water line.

Hollow seas Waves so disturbed by shoals or currents as to form

higher crests and deeper hollows as the distance between each decreases.

Hollow ended Having fine lines at bow and stern.

Holystone A block of sandstone used for scouring a wet deck.

Home The correct place for anything, eg sheet home, ram home, etc.

Homeward bound Returning to home port or country.

Homeward bound stitches Extra long stitches used when clothes, sails, etc, are repaired in a hurry.

Hong Kong buoy A buoy through which a chain can be pulled for securing purposes, the ring on the chain being kept afloat by the buoy, which has no other use.

Hoods The end planks fore and aft.

Hook The anchor.

Hooker, hookpot A term of affection or derision for a ship.

Hookrope A general utility length of rope fitted with a hook.

Hoops Bands of wood fitted round a sailing boat's mast, to retain the luff and facilitate hoisting and lowering the sail.

Horizon The circle bounding that part of the earth's surface visible from any one point. The higher it is viewed from the more distant it is.

Horn timber The piece of wood joining the keel to the transom, at an angle, in a yacht.

Horning The process of setting up the frames.

Horny, horn-fisted, 'orney Possessing tough hands, and a character to match, through hard work and experience.

Horse A metal bar fitted athwartships in sailing boats which retains the main sheet and on which it travels (see also **Fore horse**, p 72). A sand bar that the tide may leave high and dry.

Horse market Tidal races.

Horsing Caulking (see p 36).

Hounding That part of a mast from the deck to the stayband or hounds.

Hounds Wooden shoulders or staybands at the masthead of sailing boats on which the trestle trees or shrouds rest.

Hour glass A pair of glass bulbs joined to each other by a narrow neck, hollowed to permit sand, mercury, etc, to pass from one to the other in a specified time interval (now obsolete).

House Place, rest, or secure anything in its proper place.

House a mast Lower it in the fids, or lash it up and down to a lower mast, without 'sending it down'.

Houseflag The private flag of an owner, shipping line, or company.

Houseline Three strands of hemp tarred and loosely made up into soft handy line for lashings, seizings, etc.

Housewife, hussif A small roll-up receptacle used by seamen to keep needles, cottons, scissors, and sewing gear together.

Housing That part of a mast from its heel to the upper deck.

Hove to Under way but not making way through the water.

Hove to under bare poles Hove to in bad weather, with no canvas set.

Hovercraft A modern amphibious craft; when under way it skims over the surface instead of on it, sustained by a cushion of air.

Hoy A large single-deck boat, usually sloop-rigged. A small vessel used for transportation to and from a ship close inshore.

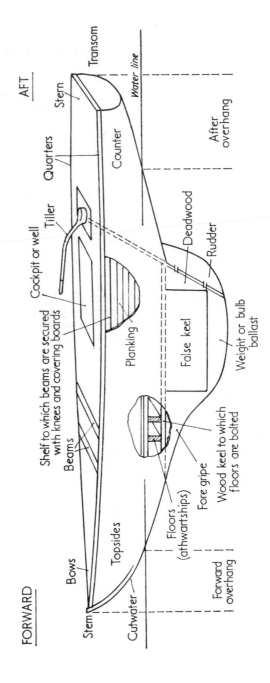

FORWARD

Bows

Topsides

Stem

Cutwater

Forward overhang

Floors (athwartships)

Fore gripe

Wood keel to which floors are bolted

Beams

Shelf to which beams are secured with knees and covering boards

Cockpit or well

Tiller

Planking

False keel

Weight or bulb ballast

Deadwood

Rudder

AFT

Transom

Water line

Stern

Counter

Quarters

After overhang

Principal parts of a hull (small yacht)

Hug the coast or **land**   Keep as near as possible along a coast.

Hulk   The body of a ship. An old ship unfit for further use at sea.

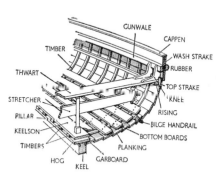

TIMBER
THWART
STRETCHER
PILLAR
KEELSON
TIMBERS
HOG
KEEL
GARBOARD
PLANKING
BOTTOM BOARDS
BILGE HANDRAIL
RISING
KNEE
TOP STRAKE
RUBBER
WASH STRAKE
CAPPEN
GUNWALE

Parts of a hull (small boat)

Hull   The structural frame, with planking or plating, forming the body of a ship.

Hull down   Said of a vessel beyond the horizon with masts only in view.

Hurricane   A violent wind storm, originating in the West Indies.

Hydrofoil   A boat so constructed that when running she is carried by and on immersed wings, with her hull clear of the water.

Hydroglider   A type of boat designed with airscrews as its main means of propulsion.

Hydrography   The science of surveying the seashore, rivers, and large areas of water for the preparation of charts.

Hydroplane   A small motor-driven craft that skims along at high speed without taking off.

Ice yacht   A specially made wooden skeleton-frame, triangular or cross-shaped and fitted with steel runners and sails, for use when racing or sailing across ice.

Icebound   Prevented from making way owing to formation of ice. Applied also to a place affected by such conditions.

In ballast   Carrying no cargo.

In company   Describes two or more ships keeping with each other.

In irons   Said of a sailing boat that has come head to wind, when she has no way and will not fill on either tack.

In stays   A sailing vessel is said to be 'in stays' when going from one tack to the other through the wind, ie 'going about'.

In the clear   A relative term describing the width or length of the bow of a shackle, eg 'wide in the clear' or 'long in the clear'.

In the jaw Used to describe the cant of a rope; when laid up hard and tight, it is said to be 'short in the jaw'; while soft, loosely laid, and much used rope is usually 'long in the jaw'.

In the offing Standing off shore. Not far away.

In the wind's eye Dead into a strong wind.

Inboard Within the framework of a ship. Nearer towards amidships.

Inclinometer See **Clinometer**, p 41.

Inflated bags Air-bags of varying shapes and sizes used to provide dinghies with additional buoyancy.

Inhaul The rope used to recover or haul in anything that has been hauled outboard, eg as a traveller on a sounding boom, etc.

Innards A vessel's interior. The inside of anything.

In-rigger A boat that has its rowlocks on the gunwale.

Inshore On or near the shore. Towards the shore.

Inshore tack A vessel working to windward when sailing along a coast will 'stand in' towards it from seaward on the inshore tack; when she goes about and 'stands out' to sea, she is 'making an offing'.

Insurance hawser A towing hawser kept reeled ready for emergency use, as stipulated by an insurance policy clause.

Inter-cardinal points The half cardinals (see p 83).

Intermediate points The three-letter points (see p 162) on a compass card.

Internal bound or **strapped** Applied to blocks with a metal frame within the shell to support the pin.

International class boats Yachts and dinghies designed to compete on an international basis and granted international status by the International Yacht Racing Union.

International code of signals The system of signals adopted for use between ships and shore stations of all nations, with simplicity of use in coding and decoding in any language.

Inwales Inboard fore-and-aft strengtheners of the hull.

Irish pennants Small ends of line, frayed ends, yarns, etc, left anywhere aloft and making a ship look untidy.

Irishman's reef The head of a sail tied up or knotted.

FLAGS OF THE INTERNATIONAL CODE OF SIGNALS

THEIR MEANING WHEN ANY ONE IS HOISTED SINGLY

(The Morse code sign for each letter is shown on the right)

A I have a diver down. Keep well clear at slow speed   (· —)

B I am taking on, or discharging, or carrying dangerous
   goods
               (— · · ·)

C Yes (affirmative)   (— · — ·)

D Keep clear of me, I am manoeuvring with difficulty   (— · ·)

E I am altering my course to starboard   (·)

F I am disabled. Communicate with me   (· · — ·)

G I require a pilot   (— — ·)

H I have a pilot on board   (· · · ·)

I I am altering my course to port   (· ·)

J I am on fire and have dangerous cargo on board. Keep
   well clear of me
               (· — — —)

K I wish to communicate with you   (— · —)

L You should stop your vessel instantly   (· — · ·)

M My vessel is stopped and making no way through the
   water
               (— —)

N No (negative)   (— ·)

O Man overboard   (— — —)

P All persons are to repair on board, as the vessel is about
   to proceed to sea
               (· — — ·)

Q My vessel is healthy and I request free pratique   (— — · —)

R *This letter has not been allocated a meaning*   (· — ·)

S My engines are going full speed astern   (· · ·)

T Do not pass ahead of me   (—)

U You are standing into danger   (· · —)

V I require assistance   (· · · —)

W I require medical assistance   (· — —)

X Stop carrying out your intentions and watch for my
   signals
               (— · · —)

Y I am dragging my anchor   (— · — —)

Z I require a tug   (— — · ·)

NB. Flags G, P & Z may have different meanings when used by fishing vessels; flags K and S have special meanings as landing signals for small boats with crews or persons in distress.

Iron wire rope Non-flexible wire rope used only for heavy standing rigging.

Ironbound A rugged coast of high rocks with no safe anchorage.

Isherwood construction The build of a ship in which the main framing sections run fore and aft and not athwartships.

Isobar A line drawn to link areas of equal barometric pressure.

Isogonic line A line drawn on a chart to illustrate where the stated variation is a constant factor.

Isotherm A line drawn on a chart to join areas of equal temperature.

Jack, the The Union flag. The flag of any country hoisted on a staff in the bows, before all; not to be confused with colours (see p 45).

Jackass The bag or plug for a hawse pipe, to prevent water entering.

Jackass a boom Change a spinnaker boom from one side to the other.

Jackass rig A three-masted schooner with square sails set on her

96

foremast; thus a 'jackass schooner' has no main topmast.

Jackrope The lacing used to bend on the foot of a boomed mainsail.

Jackstaff The staff right forward on which the jack is flown.

Jackstay A wire rope to carry a traveller, or to which a sail, awning, etc, may be secured. A rod or rope affixed to a yard to which a sail may be bent.

Jackyard A small boom to extend a spinnaker topsail when racing.

Jacob's ladder A portable rope or wire ladder, with wooden rungs or slats, used on booms, over the stern, for going aloft, etc.

Jags The term applied to old rope, 'stopped up' in 5 fathom bights or 'jags' for disposal.

Jamie Green A sail set under the jib-boom to the dolphin striker.

Jaw of a rope The distance along a rope that includes all its strands once, ie one turn or twist of a strand.

Jawrope The rope joining the jaws of a gaff to keep it to the mast; often threaded through perforated balls, to move easily.

Jaws The semi-circular horns of a gaff which engage the mast.

Jaws of a block The space in the shell where the sheave revolves.

Jaws of a shackle The space between the lugs.

Jetsam, Jetson Goods thrown overboard to lighten a vessel.

Jettison Throw overboard, especially in time of danger.

Jetty A projection, pier, or wharf constructed for use of shipping.

Jewel block One with a grommet head, used when hoisting studding sails.

Jew's harp An anchor shackle.

Jib The foremost sail in a sailing vessel, triangular in shape, and set between the foremasthead and the bowsprit; in larger ships there are three—the inner and outer set on the stays of the jib-boom and the outermost 'flying jib' set on the stay of the 'flying' jib-boom. There are many special jibs used for racing.

Jib netting Network under a jib-boom to stop men and sails going overboard.

Jib stick A small spar, spiked at one end and fitted with a jaw at the other, for spreading a jib, especially when goose-winging.

Jib topsail A light triangular sail

set above the jib; it is hanked to the topmast stay and sometimes called 'jib o' jib'.

Jibber One who has second thoughts about attempting something, and then refuses to make the effort.

Jib-boom An extension of a bowsprit, used for setting the jib.

Jib-club A small boom used on the foot of a foresail or jib.

Jib-headed rig Any rig of which all the sails are triangular.

Jib-header A thimble-headed gaff topsail shaped like a jib.

Jiggamaree A makeshift substitute used in an unseamanlike manner.

Jigger A small handy deck tackle, with one single and one double block, fitted with rope from 2 to 3in (see **Tackles**, p 163).

Jiggermast The after mast in any four- or five-masted ship. Sometimes also applied to the after mast in yawls and ketches.

Jill about Idle around, wasting time; going nowhere or doing nothing particular.

Jingles Nautical mnemonics (aids to memory) in verse form. There

G

are many relating to weather, steering, etc, of which the following are the most popular and are worth memorising:

When both side lights you see ahead,
Port your tiller and show your red;
But green to green, or red to red,
Means perfect safety—go ahead.

If to your starboard red appear,
It is your duty to keep clear;
To act as judgement says is proper,
To port—or starboard—back—or
    stop her.

But when upon your port is seen
A steamer's starboard light of green,
There's not so much for you to do,
For green to port keeps clear of you.

Both in safety and in doubt
Always keep a good look out;
In danger, with no room to turn,
Ease her, stop her, go astern.

Jockeying The period before a sailing race when all entrants assemble behind the starting-line, where they 'jockey' around, stop watch in hand, seeking to obtain a favourable position.

Jog along Going slowly intentionally. A sailing boat with foresheet hauled to windward and main sheet payed off, with helm down, will make very little headway; a useful method when it is necessary to wait.

Joggle shackle A bent elongated shackle fitted with a quick-release pin; used for passing cable round the stem when mooring.

Joining shackle The type of shackle used to join together the many lengths of cable (each of which is also called a shackle) to make a continuous chain.

Jolly boat A boat carried or used for general utility work.

Journal Any kind of log or record written up, officially or otherwise.

Jumbo A boom used as a club to a forestaysail.

Jump the gun Perform an act before the stipulated time (from crossing the line in sailing races before the gun is fired).

Jumper stay Any kind of preventer stay or chain, used as a martingale.

Jumping ladder A light rope ladder used for manning a seaboat or placing over the side.

Jumping ship All hands jumping together to move a boat that has run aground. Deserting a ship, with intent, before it sails.

Junk Old or condemned cordage, canvas, or other gear of no further use for service.

Jury anchor A heavy weight used in lieu of an anchor in emergency.

Jury mast A temporary mast or

boom, erected and rigged up as a replacement for one that has 'gone by the board', or 'carried away'.

Jury rig Any temporary device rigged up, especially to spread sail.

Jury rudder A temporary steering arrangement made or set up when the rudder is lost or unusable.

Jute heart The core or heart of a rope, usually of jute.

Jybe A variant of gybe (see p 82).

Kapok Light buoyant material for filling bedding and life-jackets.

Kayak A canoe made of sealskin stretched on a frame.

Keckling Protection for a large rope or cable made by binding it spirally with old rope, wormed in the lay and sometimes served over.

Kedge A small auxiliary anchor carried by large ships for warping without raising steam, or for keeping steady in a required position.

Kedge, to To move a ship by laying out the kedge, eg when working in a confined channel, etc.

Keel The fore-and-aft plate or timber, the backbone of a ship, from stem to stern, upon which the hull

is built up; the foundation at the middle line of a ship's bottom. A small low flat-bottomed lighter. A ship generally.

Keel, to To keel a boat is to turn her keel upwards.

Keelson An inner keel fitted over the floor timbers to bind them to the keel.

Keep a good hold of the land, keep the land aboard Hug the coast (see p 93).

Keep a good offing Keep well offshore when sailing, so as to be clear of danger should the wind shift to blow onshore.

Keep away Put the helm up. Keep off.

Keep her full Keep the sails drawing.

Keep the sea Remain outside and not enter a port, for any reason.

Keep your luff Order to the helmsman to keep her close to the wind.

Keep your weather eye lifting Keep a special lookout.

Keeping her sheer Refers to a vessel lying to a single anchor that swings clear, with the tide, and avoids fouling her anchor.

99

Keeping stroke   Rowing together with precision.

Kentledge   Pig iron, as laid out in a vessel for ballast.

Ketch   A two-masted sailing vessel, somewhat resembling a yawl (see p 176), but with a larger mizzen stepped well before her rudder.

Kevels   Raised ends of timbers, or other vertical pieces of wood, to which ropes may be belayed.

Kick   The movement of a vessel's stern when helm or power is suddenly applied.

Kicking straps   Rope lanyards to prevent a boom rising when sailing.

Killick   A small anchor. A large stone or weight used for anchoring.

Kingplank   The centre main plank of any deck.

Kingpost   A vertical post, sometimes resembling a mast, erected near the hatches to support and top a derrick boom.

Kingspoke   The midship spoke (see p 115).

Kingston valve   A valve controlling an aperture in a ship's bottom.

100

Kink   A twist in a rope that will prevent it running or coiling freely.

Kisbie, kisbey   The common circular lifebuoy of cork sewn in canvas.

Kitchen rudder   One comprising two curved blades that may completely enclose the propeller. It is rotated by a wheel on the tiller to open or close for going either ahead or astern; the direction and speed are thus controlled from the tiller, while the engine runs unattended at one speed.

Kite   Light lofty sail.

Kite drag   Cross spars and canvas, rigged like a kite and weighted at the tail, for use as a drogue.

Knees   End supports to cross fittings such as thwarts, beams, etc. In boats they are of specially grown and shaped wood. A 'hanging knee' is vertical and a lodging knee' is horizontal. The 'knee of the head' is the support for a figurehead (see p 66).

Knight heads   Timbers each side of the bow to support the bowsprit. From this term comes 'heads' for the latrines built therein.

Knockabout   Formerly a sloop with the forestay led to the bow at a time when bowsprits were being discarded; now any boat that is used for various purposes.

Knockdown The 'blow' that capsizes any small sailing craft.

Knot A nautical measure of speed —1 nautical mph. In a reference to speed the words 'per hour' are not used, as they are incorporated in the meaning of the word 'knot'. Formerly a division of the log line, marked by knots, to determine speed. A way of using a loop or combination of loops to fasten a rope to another or any object, or to make the end of a rope larger.

Knots and splices The shaping of ropes for various uses; often referred to as 'marline-spike seamanship' (see p 113).

Knuckle An angle or sharp change of contour in a timber or frame.

Knuckle mast One that is hinged to lower inboard.

Labour Pitch and roll in heavy seas; show signs of 'working' (see p 175).

Lacing A length of line used to bend on sails, screens, dodgers, etc.

Lady's ladder Shrouds that are rattled too closely.

Lagan, ligan Goods sunk at sea and marked with a buoy for recovery. Goods found in a wreck or sunk vessel on the bottom.

Lagging Said of the tide when the interval between successive tides is above the average, and the time of high water is retarded. A sluggish compass card is said to 'lag' in its movement (the term 'keep the compass afloat' is used when it appears sluggish). Material used for insulating pipes, etc.

Laid up Refers to the way strands are wound together to make a rope, ie right- or left-handed, or if long or short 'in the jaw' (see p 94). A ship not in commission or afloat; out of use.

Landfall Approaching land, especially after a long voyage. To 'make a good landfall' is to arrive at the spot anticipated.

Landing stage A flat platform, usually on pontoons, for disembarkation.

Landing strake The upper strake but one on each side of a boat.

Landings, lands The overlapping edges of planking, as in clinker-built boats.

Landlubber A man of the land who is uninitiated into nautical matters.

Landmark A conspicuous object on shore used as a navigational aid.

Lanyard A rope rove through

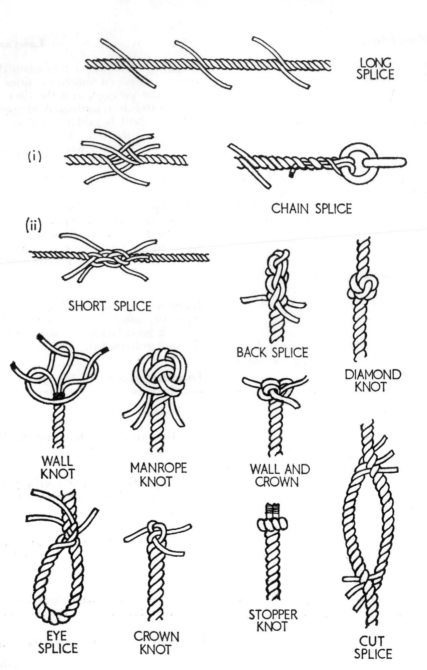

LONG SPLICE

(i)

CHAIN SPLICE

(ii)

SHORT SPLICE

BACK SPLICE

DIAMOND KNOT

WALL KNOT

MANROPE KNOT

WALL AND CROWN

EYE SPLICE

CROWN KNOT

STOPPER KNOT

CUT SPLICE

Knots and splices

Lap

Lay a ship by the lee

dead eyes to set up the shrouds. A small line or rope used to sling or attach anything.

Lap A leg of a sailing course. A complete circuit or any defined part of it; hence the 'last lap', meaning the final effort or distance.

Lap ahead, get a Complete preparations in advance of an event, or gain advantage by forethought.

Lap ahead—walk back To have got a 'lap ahead' and then discover it is to no purpose.

Lap-jointed, lap-straked Describes the system of planking as used in clinker-built boats.

Large Sailing large (see **Sail large,** p 140).

Lash down Secure anything firmly by means of a lashing.

Lash the helm, tiller, or **wheel** Secure it by rope in the required position.

Lash-up Anything untidily put together or insecurely lashed.

Lashing A rope suitable for securing anything in position or making it fast, by binding it taut to prevent movement.

Lask along Sail free and fast with a quartering wind.

Lasket A loop of line at the foot of a sail to which an extra sail may be fastened.

Last dog Alternative name for the second dog watch (see p 56).

Lateen A large triangular or four-sided fore-and-aft sail, with a very short luff, bent to a yard that is set obliquely to the mast.

Latitude The position of a place in relation to the Equator, measured in degrees north or south.

Launch An extra large boat propelled by oars, sail, steam, or motor; The name is also applied to some small power boats.

Launch, to To move a vessel from the land to the water and float her.

Launching ways The bed of timbers along which a ship slides when being launched.

Lay, lie, laying, lying The similarity of these words has made them almost synonymous in common usage.

Lay, to To come or to go (with appropriate direction).

Lay aboard Come alongside.

Lay a ship by the lee Run off the wind, and bring it round on to the

103

lee quarter, until the sails are laid aback.

Lay back Apply one's full weight to anything, as in rowing.

Lay days The number of days allowed a charter party for shipping or unshipping cargo.

Lay down The order to descend from aloft.

Lay her course Said when a ship points the mark she is making for.

Lay of a rope The direction, right- or left-handed, in which the tightly twisted strands are laid up round each other to make a rope.

Lay off Keep clear. A directive to a boat to wait away from a gangway.

Lay off a course Work out a proposed course on a chart.

Lay out a kedge Send a kedge and hawser by boat, so that they may be slipped for warping or shifting (kedging) ship.

Lay out the cable 'Range' the cable by placing it lengthwise for examination or other purpose, or to prevent kinking.

Lay the land Cause the land to disappear over the horizon by sailing away from it.

Lay up Berth a vessel out of service. To lay up yarns or strands is to twist them tightly and form a rope.

Lay to Stop by keeping in the wind.

Layers Variable frictional layers or belts of water along the side of a moving vessel. The 'inner layer' and 'laminar layer' both act to advantage when a hull is smoothed down, as for racing.

Laying along A ship that is kept pressed down sideways by the wind.

Laying off Method of developing a ship's form on the mould-loft floor.

Lazarette A small provision store right forward or aft. A ship or place used for quarantine cases.

Lazy guy A small rope or tackle to prevent the spanker boom swaying.

Lazy painter A small additional painter in a boat, used to bend on to a boom ladder so that the boat may be hauled to the ladder during manning.

Lazyjacks Ropes from a boom to the mast to help in gathering in a sail when lowering it.

Lead The lead of a rope is the direction it takes. The weight attached to a line for taking soundings.

Lead line The line used for soundings (see **Hand lead and line**, p 84).

Leader cable A transmitting cable laid on the bottom in a fairway or channel to assist certain vessels to keep over it.

Leading block Any block used to guide the fall of a tackle.

Leading mark, landing mark A distinguishable mark or object on the land that may be used as a guide for navigational purposes.

Leading part That part of a tackle that is pulled to overhaul it.

Leadsman The seaman who heaves the lead to take soundings.

Leak An opening, chink, or crack that lets water in.

Lee Shelter from the wind. As a prefix, it means the opposite to 'weather'.

Lee helm The helm when 'down'. A boat tending to turn to leeward would need lee helm to keep her up.

Lee shore The shore facing the lee side of a ship, on to which the wind would drive her if she were unable to make an offing.

Lee side The opposite side from the direction of the wind.

Leeboards Large wooden boards suspended over the side of flat-bottomed boats, the lee one being lowered to reduce leeway on a wind.

Leebowing A racing tactic in which the 'give way' boat goes about on the lee bow of another and thus 'backwinds' her competitor.

Leebowing the tide A sailing advantage secured by taking the tide on the lee bow whenever possible in going to windward.

Leech The after edge of a four-sided fore-and-aft sail. Both side edges of a square sail.

Leech line In large sailing ships the line from a leech for use as a brail. In smaller boats a light line held loosely on the leech of jib or mainsail, to adjust the curvature of the sail.

Leech rope That part of the bolt-rope sewn on to a leech.

Lee-O The helmsman's warning to a crew before going about.

Leeward (pronounced 'looard') The direction in which the wind blows. Down wind.

Leeward, get to Get on the wrong side or fall foul of anyone or anything. Lose out on any venture.

Leeway The angular distance between a sailing ship's fore-and-aft line and the direction actually made good; as a distance, it refers to the amount she is driven to leeward of her course by the wind.

Leeway, make up Make up lost time or ground.

Left bank (of a river or stream) The left side when one is looking downstream.

Left-handed rope Rope laid up in the opposite way to 'right-handed rope' (see p 135). It should be coiled anticlockwise.

Leg The side of a sailing race course between two marks.

Leg-of-mutton rig Triangular mainsails.

Legs Upright wooden spars placed to keep a boat upright when she takes the ground.

Let draw Let the wind take the weather sheet over and trim the lee one.

Let fly Let the sheet go, suddenly spilling the wind from a sail.

Let go Cast off, or release anything; 'letting go with a run' means suddenly releasing a rope holding a weight, which will 'take charge' and overhaul the rope at great speed.

Let things ride Make no change.

Lie on your oars Cease pulling and remain seated with oars in a horizontal position. Have a rest from work.

Lie to Keep a ship as steady as possible in a gale, reducing sail to a minimum to meet the heavy seas.

Lifebelt A belt worn to give buoyancy in water; it may be filled with cork or kapok, or inflated by air. When worn as a garment, the appliance is termed a life-jacket.

Lifeboat All boats carried by any vessel are primarily for lifesaving in emergency; shore-based lifeboats are maintained around our coasts to assist any vessel in distress in the vicinity.

Lifebuoy A buoy capable of supporting a person in the water.

Lifting sail One that tends to lift the bows, eg jib.

Lifts Ropes from a mast to suspend the ends of its yardarms.

Light along Move, lift, or carry in a certain direction.

Light to Fleet a rope back quickly after a haul, for turning up.

Light vessel, lightship A stationary vessel carrying a distinguishing mark and lights, as an aid to navigation.

Light waterline The draught at which a ship floats when empty of all dead weight.

Lighter A large non-propelled open boat for loading and unloading cargo from large ships.

Limber A channel on each side of the keelson, for drainage.

Limber chain A length of small chain kept rove through limber holes and used for wriggling away blockages.

Limber holes Small gutters between the planking and timbers, in the bottom of a boat, for draining water aft to pump or bail out.

Limp home Return at reduced speed because of some mishap.

Line A small rope capable of many specific functions, each with its descriptive prefix, eg gantline, heaving line, etc. Some are also described by their weight, and others by their functions in fishing.

Line ahead, abeam, or astern Applied to several ships in company so positioned or dispersed when under way.

Line of transit A guide line drawn

on a chart to indicate a passage through a fairway, clear of dangers.

Liner A large steam- or motorship of a shipping line.

Lines of a ship Her outlined form, as shown on the drawings.

Lines of flotation Horizontal markings of the Plimsoll mark (see p 126).

Link A ring of a chain cable.

Liquid compass A bowl in which the card floats on a mixture, usually 50 per cent alcohol and 50 per cent distilled water.

List An inclination to one side.

Lizard A wire or rope pennant fitted with an eye, for a rope to be rove through or made fast to.

Lloyd's The London Association of Underwriters which classifies vessels according to various specifications, to be found in *Lloyd's Register of Shipping* and *Lloyd's Register of Yachts*.

Loadline The Plimsoll mark also called 'load water line' (LWL).

Local attraction Compass error caused by the magnetic attraction of cranes, machinery, piers, or ironstone in a ship's vicinity.

107

Lock An enclosure for a ship. Part of a waterway between gates to enable a vessel to transfer to a different level.

Loft The sail loft or moulding loft on shore.

Log A piece of wood or metal used with a long line, or any other apparatus, for measuring a ship's speed and progress.

Log, to To enter or record in the log book all principal events connected with the ship and its working.

Log book, log The book in which are recorded all references to weather and navigation, log readings, work done, and other events of importance. A rough working log is kept on the bridge and signed after each watch, while a smooth, fair or abstract copy is written up later.

Log glass An instrument similar to the hour glass which runs out in 28 seconds; it is used with the log-ship.

Log towing Logs are towed wide end (butt) first, with a timber hitch round the narrow end, and a half hitch at the towing end.

Logchip, logship A wooden quadrant, weighted on the curve so that it floats upright, and fitted with a bridle span to secure to the logline; when streamed it remains vertical, broadside to, as the ship moves on, thus enabling her speed to be counted in knots by use of the log glass. A slight jerk will release one of the bridle ropes, which is only pegged in to facilitate recovery.

Loggerhead A small bollard with arms, for securing a rope.

Logline A rope of plaited flax for towing the rotator of a patent log; formerly marked with a knot at every 50ft for timing a ship's speed with the 28 second log glass.

Long board A sailing vessel is on her 'long board' when sailing the longest leg on the most favourable tack.

Long fetch To sail close hauled between two widely separated points without having to go about is to make a 'long fetch'.

Long in the jaw, long jawed Describes a rope well stretched, with a tendency to untwist, after considerable use and strain.

Long leg The most favourable tack used in a beat to windward. Any sailing vessel that draws a lot of water is said to have a 'long leg'.

Long splice A method of joining two ropes together where they are to be rove through a block. The ends are unlaid well back and butted together with the strands married one of the strands is unlaid back and a strand from the other rope laid up in its place; one strand is likewise unlaid in the reverse direction, and its lay occupied as before, leaving three well separated pairs of ends, each of which is half hitched together and then tucked over and under to form a neat finish.

Long stay When the anchor is at some distance from the ship, with the cable on or just off the bottom.

Longboat The name once given to the largest and strongest boat of a ship.

Longitude The position (in degrees) of any place east or west of Greenwich, or any other meridian.

Loof The narrowing of a vessel's beam towards the stern.

Lookout Man specially posted to keep diligent watch, to observe and report all ships, lights, and other objects that come into view.

Loom The inboard rounded handle-grip of an oar.

Looming Showing up large. Indistinct appearance through fog.

Loose-footed Applied to a sail not laced to a boom.

Lose way Make less progress.

Loud hailer A short-distance microphonic megaphone.

Low water The lowest level reached by the tide.

Low water, in With little water under. Short of money.

Lower and dip An order given in a dipping lug cutter when going about: the foresail is lowered sufficiently to unhook the tack, swing the whole sail round abaft the mast, and reset it the other side.

Lower away 'Start the falls' when lowering a boat or working a tackle.

Lower boom The long spar projecting from the ship's side in harbour for boats not in use to secure to; it is fitted with boatropes, lizards, and a Jacob's ladder.

Lower deck The deck below a main deck. Used in the navy as a collective term for ratings of all messes.

Lower handsomely Ease a rope so as to lower gradually.

Lower mast In a built mast the first section from the deck; above it come the topmast, topgallantmast, and royal mast.

Lubber A clumsy unseamanlike person.

Lubber's hole The space in the top, at the mast, through which lubbers may pass to avoid using the futtock rigging as sailors should.

Lubber's line A black line marked inside a compass bowl to denote the ship's head direction as read from the card.

Lubber's points Two black lines marked in a compass bowl, one the lubber's line and the other opposite it.

Lubber's trademark The end of a rope left with its strands unwhipped.

Luff The fore edge of a four-sided fore-and-aft sail. A tackle with a double block and a single one, rove with rope 3in or larger (see **Tackles**, p 163).

Luff, to To put the helm down and bring the boat's head closer to the wind.

Luff alee A helm order meaning hard alee.

Luff and lie Luff and shake, and keep her there.

Luff and shake, luff and touch her See how near to the wind the ship can be brought.

Luff up Put the helm down to bring her up to the wind. A 'luffing

match' is an attempt to outwit a racing rival by frequently luffing up.

Luff upon luff A method of gaining increased purchase by hooking the block of one luff to the hauling part of another luff.

Lug, lugsail A fore-and-aft sail, almost square in shape, bent to a yard and slung to leeward of the mast when hoisted and set, with its tack well forward. Used in various rigs, and referred to as a standing, dipping, or balanced lug.

Lugger A vessel, especially a fishing boat, fitted with lugsails.

Lying alongside Waiting at or secured to a jetty or pier, as distinct from being at anchor. At a gangway.

Lying to See **Lie to**, p 106.

Made mast A ship's mast made of several pieces bound and rounded off.

Mae West A large spinnaker. An inflatable air-tube worn around the body to provide a self-carried life-belt. A life-jacket.

Magnetic bearing The bearing of an object in relation to the magnetic meridian.

Magnetic compass A ship's standard compass, used for determining the magnetic meridian.

Magnetic course A course as read from the magnetic rose, ie the true course with variation applied to it.

Magnetic meridian The line in which a freely suspended compass needle will rest when free of all local attraction.

Magnetic north The northern centre of the earth's magnetic influence (as distinct from the true north). It is approx 70° N and 97° 30′ W.

Main A prefix denoting the principal object of several similar ones.

Main boom The spar used for extending the foot of a fore-and-aft mainsail.

Main brace The purchase attached to a main yard for trimming it to the wind.

Main deck The main deck of a ship's structure, extending fore and aft the whole length of the ship.

Main derrick The largest in a ship, for hoisting boats, etc.

Main sheet The tackle by which a mainsail is trimmed when sailing.

Main stay The rope stretching forward from the main masthead and supporting it.

Main top The platform erected at the mainmasthead (see **Top**, p 165).

Main yard The lower yard to which a mainsail is bent.

Mainmast The tallest and principal mast of a ship.

Mainsail The large sail hoisted on a mainmast. In sailing boats a 'boom mainsail' has the foot extended by a boom, and a 'gaff mainsail' has its head extended and laced to a gaff.

Make Get somewhere or attain something.

Make fast Belay (a rope). Secure (a boat to a boom, ladder, etc).

Make headway Advance through the water; progress.

Make sail Set the sails; increase the sail area.

Make sternway Move through the water stern first; go backwards.

Make the land Approach to within sight of the coast.

Make water Leak.

Making A tide is said to be making when 'coming on' (see p 45).

Mal de mer Seasickness.

Man, mann Provide a crew for (a vessel or boat); place people where required for any purpose or duty.

Man overboard The alarm call raised by *anyone* who sees someone fall over the side into the water.

Man the falls, capstan, boat, etc. An order passed to take up the position indicated, in readiness to operate or use anything.

Manger The small space in the bows between the hawse pipes, fitted with a high coaming to keep water from flowing along the deck. Formerly the pen in which livestock were kept.

Manhole An entrance into a compartment specifically constructed to enable one person to enter for inspection, etc.

Manila Rope made from fibres of the abaca banana plant, from the Philippines; it is not tarred as it does not rot in sea water.

Manoeuvre Skilful management of a boat in a tricky situation.

Manrope A line rigged to assist someone climbing a ladder.

Manrope knot A fancy but practical knot on the end of a manrope,

to hang or retain it at the eye of a stanchion.

Marconi rig A sailing rig with a jib-headed mainsail set to a tall curved mast with an elaborate staying system; so named because it resembles a wireless mast.

Marine A comprehensive term embodying a country's nautical affairs.

Marine growth Barnacles, weeds, etc, that grow on a ship's bottom.

Marine stores All items, from movable fittings to all provisions and other necessities, that a ship may need to carry.

Mariner A sailor, navigator, or seaman, who, in any rank or capacity, earns his living on the sea.

Mariner's splice A long splice put into cable-laid rope; it is made in the ordinary way, but finished off with the strands of each rope unlaid and tucked in.

Maritime Relating to shipping or the sea.

Mark Any object that may be useful for the guidance of shipping. A depth marked on a leadline (see **By the mark**, p 32).

Marker buoy Any type of distinguishable buoy placed in position to mark anything, eg those laid out for sailing races, etc.

Marl, to   To pass a whipping or serving about a rope, with every turn knotted in case of damage by chafing.

Marline   Small line of two hemp strands loosely laid up.

Marline spike   A pointed tapered iron spike used for opening the strands of rope when splicing.

Marline-spike hitch   A quick handy hitch made by laying a spike through a jamming bight, to use it for leverage.

Marline-spike seamanship   A term embracing knotting, splicing, seizing, stropping blocks, etc; the art of shaping and working ropes.

Marling hitch   Used when a long lashing is used to marl down sails, hammocks, etc; made by passing a rope over and under in a half hitch, making an overhand knot round all, and repeating.

Marry   Join two ropes by butting the unlaid ends together, as for splicing. Align boat's falls to hoist them together.

Martingale   A guy fitted down from a spar or boom to stop it lifting.

Mast   A vertical pole, positioned by rigging, for spreading sails.

Mast clamp   A metal band hinged to a thwart to retain a mast in position.

Mast coat   A canvas band lashed round a mast at deck level, turned down and tacked to the deck, and painted to prevent a leak.

Mast hoops   Wooden hoops round a mast for the luff of a mainsail.

Mast partners   A timber framing between beams for supporting a mast.

Mast step   The recess in a boat's keelson into which a mast is stepped.

Master mariner   A Master who has passed special BOT examinations and has been awarded an MM Certificate entitling him to command a vessel.

Masthead   The top of a mast. That portion of a mast above the eyes of the rigging, or, in small boats, above the hounds.

Masthead cutter or **sloop**   A cutter or sloop whose fore stay, on which the luff of the foresail is set, reaches up to the masthead.

Masthead knot   The collar knot (see p 44); also called the jury knot.

Mastrope   The rope used for sending a mast up or down; it is rove through a sheave in the masthead, and is often used to send a man aloft in a bosun's chair.

Mate The first mate is nearly always the second in command of a ship; and second, third, and fourth mates are officers with special duties. Used also for junior assistants, eg cook's mate, etc.

Matthew Walker A knot, single or double, used to make a collar on a rope; the strands may be relaid when formed.

Mean A prefix signifying average, as in mean draught, etc.

Mean depth The depth below mean sea level.

Mediterranean gangway A gangway fitted from the stern to a jetty, the usual practice when the anchor is cast well out and the ship secures 'stern to' the jetty instead of 'lying alongside'.

Meet her A helm order to apply opposite helm to check a ship's swing.

Meet her when she shakes The order to 'meet her' as she comes round to the wind.

Menagerie racing The descriptive term for a race that includes

boats of various rigs and classes sailing under handicaps.

Mend the service Replenish or refit all worn chafing gear.

Mercator's projection A map of the world with straight parallel lines as meridians and lines of latitude; used for navigational work, it is the basis of all such charts.

Merchant shipping act The code of sea law that regulates all matters connected with British ships.

Meridian (of longitude) An imaginary circle that will cut the Equator at right-angles and pass through the poles.

Mess A number of sailors who always take their meals together at one mess table. The place where meals are consumed.

Mess deck That deck, or part of a deck, where the crew messes.

Messmate A companion who eats in the same mess.

Metre class (preceded by a figure) A classification of sailing boats and races, based on the waterline length unit.

Middle ground A shoal area that divides a fairway into two channels.

Middle ground buoys Spherical

buoys with horizontal stripes, some of which have a topmark, positioned round a middle ground.

Middle watch From midnight to 4 am. The watch on deck at that time.

Middle stitching Reinforcing weak seam by stitching along its centre.

Midship spoke The upper spoke of the wheel when the rudder is lined up fore and aft; often marked or adorned. The 'kingspoke'.

Midshipman's hitch The single blackwall hitch (see p 22) so formed on a hook that the bight also rounds the bill.

Midships The abbreviation for amidships (see p 9). Towards the centre line.

Millibar A meteorological unit of barometric pressure.

Miss stays Fail to 'go about', by getting to the wind but falling off on the same tack again.

Mitred jib One in which the cloths and seams are angled to appear as mitre joints when made up.

Mizzen, mizen The fore-and-aft sail hoisted on the mizzen-mast in a large sailing vessel; it is called the 'spanker' or 'driver', but never

referred to as a mizzensail (see also **Dandy**, p 51).

Mole A breakwater or stone pier erected to protect a harbour.

Monkey block A small single block, fitted to swivel.

Monkey gaff A small gaff hoisted or secured above the spanker gaff, for the flag.

Monkey seam, monk's seam A flat seam made by overlapping two selvages, and put in the centre of a sail when it is being made.

Monkey's fist A turk's head formed on the end of a heaving line to aid the aim; it should not be weighted or it may become a danger.

Monkey's island An elevated platform on or over the bridge.

Moonsail, moonraker A small sail set above the skyscraper.

Moor Fasten a vessel to the bottom by two anchors and cables, laid in different directions, so that she may ride by them both.

Mooring buoy A large cylindrical buoy fitted with a heavy ring to which large vessels may secure. A floating keg or other marker attached to the chain of moorings laid for small boats.

Mooring pennant The wire passed through the weather hawse pipe and round the bow to the lee one, to fetch the cable round the bow and secure it to a mooring swivel.

Mooring pipe An oval casting in the bulwarks, for passing 'fasts' (see p 65).

Mooring rights Permission to lay moorings should be obtained from the local authority; moorings laid without permission have no rights.

Mooring snatching Picking up and using any mooring without permission.

Mooring swivel A swivel-piece put in both cables when moored, to prevent the ship from getting a foul hawse.

Moorings Any layout of anchors, weights, and chains in a harbour, to which a vessel may make fast and become moored. Ships berthed alongside are frequently referred to as moored up.

Moorings in a garden, with Applies to those boats that live ashore rather than afloat, and more recently the numerous craft transported back and forth by car-trailer.

Morning watch From 4 am to 8 am

Morse code The signal code in

which letters are represented by different combinations of dots and dashes (see p 95). Whether or not one learns the Morse code, all yachtsmen should know and be able to distinguish the SOS distress signal, which can be made by foghorn, klaxon, whistle, covering and uncovering a light, or by any method, ie both audibly and visibly. It is made as one sign, with no break between the letters, thus (· · · — — — · · ·).

Morticed block One that is chiselled out of a block of wood and then fitted with a sheave; distinct from a made-up block.

Motor boat A small utility boat fitted with an inboard internal combustion engine.

Motor cruiser Term usually applied to boats up to 45ft (approx) that are fitted out for living or cruising in.

Motor dinghy A small boat, 8 to 16ft, with an inboard or outboard motor.

Motor launch Any medium-sized boat with an internal combustion engine.

Motor sailer A boat specially designed to use motor or sails, or both.

Motor ship A vessel over 200 tons, propelled by motor power.

Motor yacht   A yacht over 45ft (approx) used solely for pleasure.

Moulded hull   A hull that is built by bonding layers of veneer.

Moulding   In boat designing the depth of a piece of wood, the moulded line being the outside edge on the lines plan.

Moulds   Battens made in the mould loft for transferring the pattern from lines on the floor to the ship under construction.

Mouse   A collar of spunyarn wound on a stay to prevent a running eye passing. A mark affixed to a rope to indicate when it has reached a preselected position.

Mouse a hook   Pass a few safety turns round the neck and bill of a hook, to prevent unhooking.

Movable flukes   Possessed by any type of anchor with arms pivoted at the base.

Moving block   Term applied to the block of a tackle that hooks on to the load, as distinct from the top or stationary one.

Mud flat   A muddy shore or bank that is submerged at high tide.

Muffled oars   Oars that are bound with canvas, old clothing, etc, over the loom where they work in crutches, rowlocks, or thole pins—to deaden the noise, when this is necessary.

Mushroom   A special type of anchor, stockless and with a heavy rounded head, used for moorings laid in soft ground.

Mussel bow   Former yacht design with a cutaway forefoot and pram-like bow.

My eye and Betty Martin, all   Nonsense; lies. Said to originate from the church Latin *Mihi, beate martine.*

Naked   A ship was formerly said to be naked when her copper bottom was completely removed.

Napier's card   A method of producing a graph on a card, from which the deviation for any point may easily be read.

Narrows   The most confined part of a channel.

National class boats   Sailing boats of nationally accepted designs administered by the Royal Yachting Association (see p 137), and including such popular classes as the Swallow, Flying Fifteen, Swordfish, Redwing, Merlin-Rocket, Firefly, and Enterprise.

Nautical   Associated with ships, sea, and navigation.

Nautical almanac An Admiralty publication containing important astronomical tabulations for navigational use.

Nautical mile, sea mile A long distance measurement equal to one-sixtieth of a degree on the equator, ie 6,08oft or approx 2,000yd.

Navel pipe A pipe down through the deck by which the cable passes from the chain locker to the forecastle.

Navigation The art of determining position and directing a ship.

Navigation lights sectors A vessel's steaming lights, side lights, and overtaking light must all have their 'unobstructed visibility' sector bounded at two points ($22\frac{1}{2}°$) abaft the beam. (See diagram for description of the illuminated arcs.) Large vessels should carry a set of oil lights ready for emergency use.

Navigational aids Landmarks, buoys, calculations, or apparatus used for obtaining information to resolve chartwork.

Navigator One skilled in navigation who directs the course of a ship.

Neap tides Those with a smaller range than spring tides; they are not as high, low, or rapid.

Neaped Beneaped (see p 19).

Neck of an oar The outboard part near the blade.

Necklace A chain or rope secured round a mast or spar to hold a hanging block.

Negative buoyancy See **Buoyancy, p 31.**

Neptune's sheep Waves breaking into foam, also called 'white horses'.

Ness A cape or promontory.

Nettles Yarns of a strand when 'foxed' for pointing (see **Fox a nettle**, p 75). Reef points. Lines of a hammock clew.

Nettlestuff Small line suitable for general use.

Never let your mother say she had a jibber An encouraging phrase used when endeavouring to make someone persevere or have a go at something.

Nibbing The marginal deck planking.

Niggerheeled Said of the leech of a sail that curves inward of a line from peak to clew, and is therefore not roached (see p 136).

Nip A short turn or part of a rope caught and jammed. Seize.

Nip of a splice The part of the rope rounding the thimble.

Nipping turn Nipping one rope to another by a racking turn, so that they will travel together.

Nock The throat of a sail.

Northern lights The luminous phenomenon sometimes seen towards the north as a curtain of tremulous streams of orange light.

Northing The difference of latitude made when sailing northwards.

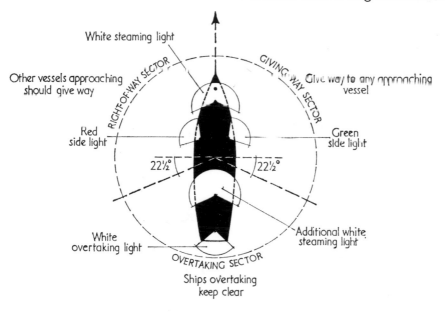

Boundaries of navigation lights sectors
NB. Side lights are not always placed abaft the steaming light

Norman A safety bar through a rudder head to prevent loss.

North A cardinal point, opposite the sun at noon.

North-east The point midway between north and east.

North-west The point midway between north and west.

Notching Joining framing timbers by halving and scarphing.

Nothing off Helm order to keep her as close to the wind or as near on course as she is, and not let her pay off.

Notice to mariners A notification published periodically for the correction of charts.

Number The number of a ship's certificate of registry.

Number board A visible indicator displayed from a yacht club showing the course of a race. An adjacent large arrow indicates the direction of the start.

Nun buoy A spar buoy fitted with various shapes more or less resembling two cones base to base.

Oakum Old hemp strands teased into loose fibres, tarred, and used for caulking.

Oar A light pole used for rowing, with a loom or handle at one end and a flat or shaped blade at the other.

Oars The order given in a rowing boat to cease pulling and 'lay on your oars', ie remain sitting upright with blades horizontal.

Observed position A vessel's position plotted on the chart from the observations of objects, as distinct from 'dead reckoning' (see p 52).

Occulting light One that is exposed for a longer period than it is obscured.

Off and on Keeping the land by 'heading in' and 'standing out'.

Off the wind Farther from the wind than necessary, if close hauled. With the wind abaft the beam and the sheets well eased.

Offshore At a distance from the shore but within the offing (see below). Applied to a wind flowing from the shore.

Officer of the day The executive officer in charge of a ship, or of any special event, eg a regatta or a race, and responsible to his superior for organisation and routine.

Offing A distance to seaward from the shore, nearer to the horizon than to the land.

Oil bag Any container that permits oil to drip out slowly to help quell the sea (hence the old adage 'to pour oil on troubled waters', meaning to smooth things out).

On a lay Said of a crew shipped on a basis of shares in lieu of wages.

On a split yarn Lightly secured, ready for immediate use or action.

On a wind, on the wind Sailing close hauled.

On the beam   At any distance from a ship at right-angles to her.

On the bow   Within the angle of 45° from right ahead, on either side.

On the quarter   On a bearing midway between abeam and astern.

On the same lay   Having a similar intent or objective.

Onboard   On or in any boat or vessel.

One design class   A group of sailing boats that conform to a standard design and are practically identical.

One two three rule   The tidal stream's normal flow of 6 hours; a method of finding the approximate strength or rise and fall during any hour, proportioned 123:321 in twelfths.

One-point bearing   Used to obtain an approximate distance from any object; bearings are taken when the object is one point before the beam and again when it is abeam, the distance run between them being multiplied by five.

Onshore   Towards the land.

Open   Said of any two marks almost in line and seen clear of each other, when one of them is not 'shut in' or hidden behind the other. Unprotected. Draw farther apart.

Open boat   One without decking or covering.

Open hawse   Riding by two anchors, with the cables clear of each other.

Orlop deck   The lowest deck, one below the lower deck.

Out of   Applied to the last port of call and not where the ship is registered or runs from.

Out of station   Not in line. The odd man out. In strange surroundings.

Out of trim   With a list or down at one end. Untidy.

Outboard   Outside a ship or boat. Farther towards a ship's side.

Outboard motor   A portable self-contained propelling unit, usually shipped over the stern of small boats.

Outer jib   The one in front of the inner jib.

Outhaul   A rope fitted to pull anything out.

Outpoint   Sail just that little bit nearer the wind than another ship.

Outrigger A projecting outboard framework built on to a float and secured to the side of a boat or canoe to counter the possibility of capsizing. A boat whose oars rest in rowlocks positioned on outboard supports. A bearing-out spar to extend sails or rigging.

Outsail, outfoot Leave another boat behind.

Outward bound Leaving a port bound for another country.

Overboard Over the side; out of the ship. To 'throw overboard' any plans, ideas, support, etc, is to withdraw them or cancel them out altogether (see also **Man overboard**, p 112).

Overfall Wave that breaks sharply over shoals or at the meeting of conflicting currents.

Overhand knot Made by passing the end of a rope over its standing part and up through the bight; used to prevent a rope unreeving.

Overhangs That part of a ship which extends over her waterline, either beyond the stem or at the sternpost.

Overhaul Sail faster than and overtake the ship ahead. Pull the blocks of a tackle farther apart to get a fresh purchase. Take apart, examine, or refit.

Overhauling whip A whip used to separate blocks of a tackle when it is 'two blocks'.

Overlap Established when an overtaking ship's bows pass the stern of the vessel being overtaken.

Overtaking light A fixed white light screened so as to be visible 12 points, ie from right astern to 2 points abaft the beam each side, and from 2 miles away; carried by all ships under way.

Overtaking vessel Any vessel approaching another within the prescribed arc of her overtaking light; also called the 'give-way' vessel. It is her duty to give way (keep clear) while the vessel she is approaching stands her course and speed.

Paddle A small light oar, short and broad, for rafts and canoes.

Paddle, to To propel a boat by hand without use of crutches, etc, or, when using oars, to pull easily with no weight applied.

Paid hand A person employed by yacht- and boat-owners, for maintenance duties and crewing.

Paint down aloft Paint a mast and yards, starting at the truck.

Painter The rope at the bow of a small boat for making it fast.

Palm The thummel. A rawhide hand band with a lead-socketed thimble, used for sailmaking. The palm, needle, and twine all come in various sizes, eg seaming palm, roping palm, etc.

Panting The vibrations of the forward plates caused by the variable resistance of the water.

Panting beam A strengthened beam fitted forward to decrease vibration.

Parallel rulers Two similar rulers attached by metal arms, and keeping parallel however they are moved; used for chartwork.

Parbuckle A purchase obtained by middling a rope and securing the bight; the ends are used to circle a cask, barrel, or other rounded object in order to roll it up an incline.

Parcel To parcel a rope is to cover it with canvas, etc, for protection; wound on as a bandage, with the lay, it is then marled down taut.

Parrel A short rope-span that attaches a yard or the jaws of a gaff, etc, to a mast; any strop or fitting used for a similar purpose.

Parrot perch A short spreader or strut on a mast to spread a stay.

Part Rope or cable is said to part when it 'carries away' (breaks).

Partners Short fore-and-aft timbers as strengthened supports between other timbers for the mast, bitts, capstan, etc, coming through a deck.

Pass Reeve through, take round, move, or transfer a rope.

Pass a stopper See **Stopper**, p 157.

Passaree A rope used with a boom to guy out square sails and keep them flat when running.

Passing The reply made when hailed at night, if not going alongside.

Patent eye A metal eye sweated on a rope end, as distinct from a splice.

Patent log A mechanical device with which a rotator is used, to work a dial indicating the distance run through the water.

Paunch mat A piece of matting easily made from several strands twisted and interwoven; used for moving heavy objects along a deck.

Pawl A short bar that lies against a toothed rack or wheel to stop a capstan, winch, etc, from 'running back' and 'taking charge'.

Pawl rack A circular cast-iron plate bedded around a capstan, secured to the deck, and notched for the pawls to work in it.

Pawl the capstan, to Drop all the pawls into position in the pawl-rack sockets, to prevent recoiling during any pause when heaving in.

Pay Run pitch into seams that have been caulked.

Pay a mast or **yard** Apply a coat of tallow, etc, as a preservative, after much use.

Pay away Pay off or fall away to leeward.

Pay down Pass a rope from aloft or to anywhere below.

Pay out Slacken and ease out a rope so that it runs freely.

Pay round Turn the ship's head.

Peak The upper corner of a sail. To peak a gaff or boom is to raise it more towards the perpendicular.

Peak span The rope support from a mast to the peak of a gaff.

Peak tanks Those compartments adjoining the stem and stern of a vessel, usually for water ballast.

Pelican The large bill-hook tongue of a screw slip.

Pelorus A pivoted metal compass dial for determining relative bearings.

Pen, penn The space between a series of piers, so built that vessels may berth four to six deep there.

Pendant, pennant A long narrow banner or triangular-shaped flag. A short length of rope with an iron thimble eye in each end, one of which is often hooked to a tackle.

Permissible factor In ship construction, the safety margin taken into consideration in the stationing of bulkheads.

Picking-up rope The rope used to secure a ship to a buoy and bring them together, so that a bridle may be put on.

Pier A staging erected to project into the sea for the use of shipping

Pig iron, pig Iron ballast in small rough bars.

Pile driver A ship tending to pitch deeply in a seaway; not being long enough to bridge two seas, she is continually being lifted and dropped violently into a trough.

Pile up Go aground.

Piles Timber or concrete supports embedded to carry the superstructure of piers, jetties, etc.

Pillar buoy A tall metal structure fixed to a buoy as a marker beacon.

Pillars Vertical supports for thwarts. Stanchions.

Pilot A person licensed to navigate ships through channels and fairways in or out of a port. A ship's navigator.

Pilot boat, cutter, or **vessel** Used by pilots for meeting any ship entering British waters.

Pilots *Admiralty Sailing Directions.*

Pinching Continually luffing too far into the wind.

Pink stern A narrowing after part with a rising sheer.

Pinnace Formerly the name for one of a warship's boats, it has been applied to steam, sailing, and pulling boats, but is now seldom used.

Pinned down Said of a boat when part of her becomes fouled and catches under a pier or other object on a rising tide.

Pintle The metal pin on a stern-post on which the rudder hangs.

Pinwheel Turn a twin-screw vessel in her own length, with one screw going ahead and the other astern.

Pipe down The order to cease work or any activity. Be quiet. Turn in.

Pitch The depression of the bows plunging into a trough in the seas. Tar and resin boiled down and used for caulking.

Pitch of a propeller The actual distance one turn would advance it in a solid medium.

Pitch-pole Be up-ended, stern first, and completely overthrown by the sea.

Planing Moving through the water with bows lifted well clear; more out of the water than in it.

Plank A length of wood for covering the outside and deck beams of ships.

Planking The outside and inside casing to the frames of a vessel, made of a series of planks or strakes.

Plastic boat A recent development in dinghy construction in which fibre glass, resin, and plastics are bonded and set in moulds.

Platform Floorboards laid over floors in small yachts to make a walking space.

Play Permissible motion occurring in the masts, frames, or any fittings.

Plimsoll mark A horizontal line bisecting a circle marked on the sides of all British merchant vessels to indicate the maximum depth to which they may be loaded.

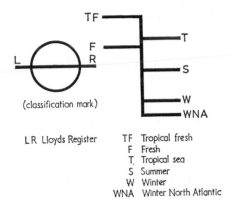

(classification mark)

L R Lloyds Register	TF	Tropical fresh
	F	Fresh
	T	Tropical sea
	S	Summer
	W	Winter
	WNA	Winter North Atlantic

Plimsoll mark and abbreviations

Plot Apply calculations to a chart.

Plug The wooden stopper that fits into the plug-hole or drain-hole of a boat. It should be secured to a lanyard.

Point A point of the compass. A projection from a coastline. A mark.

Point and graft To decorate a rope by pointing one end and working a similar pattern with the strands of the eye spliced in the other end.

Point a rope To ornament the end by unlaying to a whipping and unstranding; a tapered heart is made from the inner strands, and marled to a point, the remaining yarns being 'foxed' into nettles to make a neat sword matting pattern finish.

Point high Lay a course very close to the wind. To 'point higher' when on a wind is to sail a little closer.

Point ship To swing a ship's head to the required direction, after weighing and before proceeding.

Pointers, the Two end stars of the Great Bear. A line running through them and extended five times the distance between them would reach the Pole Star.

Points of sailing Certain angles or 'points' from the wind; each has its own relative descriptive term indicating direction and method of sailing, as compared with the wind.

Points of the compass There are thirty-two points of the compass, comprising four cardinals, four half cardinals, eight intermediates, and sixteen by-points. Each point, which is $11\frac{1}{4}°$ from its neighbour, is also subdivided into half and quarter points.

Pole mast A mast with a long head taking the place of a topmast.

Pontoon A specially designed boat,

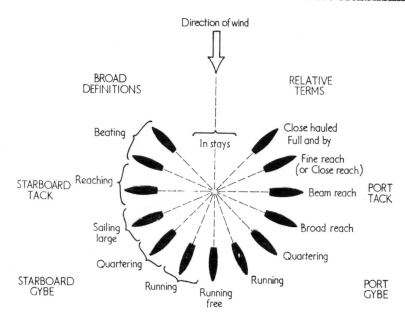

Points of sailing

similar to a scow, used to carry a roadway bridge across a stream; since an iron tank is often used to replace it, any large tank used as a platform is a pontoon.

Poop The raised deck on the after part of a ship.

Pooped If a sea breaks over the stern when a boat is running before wind or sea, she is said to be pooped.

Poppet A piece of wood used to ship into a rowlock not in use; it should be secured by a poppet lanyard to prevent its loss. A vertical

support built up to the end of a ship in construction.

Porcupine A wire in which threads have parted and jag out dangerously.

Port The left-hand side of any vessel seen from inboard looking forward. The opposite to starboard. A seaport. That part of any place that is made available for shipping. An opening in a ship's side. Carry.

Port establishment The tidal constant as tabled in the *Nautical Almanac*.

Port fire A composition made up into a slow burning signal flare.

Port sail An old sail or tarpaulin slung between ship and shore when hoisting cargo in or out.

Port tack Sailing with the wind on the port side.

Port watch The men of one watch, ie half the crew; the other half are the starboard watch.

Port-hand buoys Those marking the left-hand side of a channel seen from the entrance to the harbour, or going with the main stream of a flood tide (see **Can buoy**, p 34).

Porthole An opening in the ship's side for light and air.

Portsmouth yardstick A scale of handicap numbers allocated to various classes of racing boats to give each equal opportunity.

Position doubtful (PD) A chart notation against anything of doubtful accuracy.

Positive buoyancy The quality possessed by any craft that would allow it to remain afloat when waterlogged.

Pram A small dinghy with a cut-off bow or forward transom, used as a tender to larger boats.

Pratique Release from quarantine after the regulations have been complied with, permitting landing of goods and passengers.

Press of sail The use of all sail that can be carried.

Preventers Additional stays set up to support a mast (see **Back-stays**, p 14).

Prick a chart Mark off a course on a chart.

Prime meridian The meridian which passes through Greenwich, and from which longitude east or west is reckoned (by British seamen).

Priming Said of tides when the time between successive tides is less than average (ie 12hr 27min), thus advancing the time of high water.

Private flag An owner's flag.

Privileged vessel One having right of way and right to stand her course and speed, according to the Rule of the Road.

Prohibited area An area marked on a chart where anchoring, trawling or fishing, etc, may be forbidden by authority.

Prolonged blast A Rule of the Road definition of a blast on the siren or whistle lasting 4–6 seconds

Propeller The ship's screw; a propulsive contrivance of curved rotating blades. Large screws at slow speed are more efficient than small screws at high speed.

Protest signal A signal hoisted by a boat during a sailing race when another competitor has wronged or fouled her.

Prow The bows and fore part before the hawse pipes.

Pudding, puddening A thick padded fender fitted to a boat's bows; a thick pad of yarns or matting for use as chafing gear. A 'pudding fender' is an enclosed bundle for use over the side of yachts, etc.

Pudding chain Chain made of short links that run easily over a sheave; once used as jib halyards to avoid loss due to stretching.

Pull down Stretch and decrease in size with continual use.

Pull on a rope Haul on a rope. Heaving is an upward pull, hauling a horizontal pull, and bowsing a downward pull.

Pulpit An elevated tubular metal guard rail set up at bow and/or stern.

Punt A flat-bottomed boat suitable only for shallow inland waters; it has square ends and is propelled by pushing a pole against the bottom.

Purchase A tackle (see p 163). Leverage by any means to obtain extra power.

Put about Go on the other tack.

Put off Leave a ship in a boat.

Put the helm down (or **up**) Move the tiller to leeward (or windward).

Quadrant A navigational instrument now superseded by the sextant. The casting on a rudder head for connection to the steering gear.

Quant poles Strong poles used in small boats for canal work; they are very light, forked at one end, and 12–15ft long.

Quarantine, in Having infectious disease on board, so that contact between those onboard and the shore is prohibited.

Quarantine flag An all yellow flag displayed to indicate that the ship is in quarantine.

Quarter The side of a ship between midships and the stern.

Quarter, on the Bearing 45° abaft the beam on either side, ie on the port or starboard quarter.

Quarter deck Usually that part of the upper deck from the mainmast aft, generally reserved for the use of officers.

Quarter knees The strengthening pieces where gunwale and transom meet.

Quarter wind A wind that comes in over either quarter.

Quartering Sailing with the wind coming over the quarter.

Quartermaster The seaman whose duty it is to attend to the steering.

Quay A place for commercial shipping to berth for loading and unloading.

Queen staysail A large balloon-like sail set between masts in schooners.

Quick marks Two leading marks that are not close together but which, when used together, alter visibly after a short distance.

Quilting Meshed or interwoven rope used as a container for stone jars, etc.

Race A strong current that disturbs water over a large area.

Racing A screw is racing when it increases its revolutions as it clears the water through the boat pitching or rolling.

Racing flag A private rectangular flag hoisted when racing, instead of the burgee; it is hauled down only on retiring or when a race is completed.

Racing marks Specified objects which must be passed in correct sequence on the correct side, as ordered, and which must not be touched.

Racing rules An internationally accepted and detailed set of rules formulated to cover situations in racing when numerous craft become confined in close proximity. There are also **team racing rules**, which permit certain waiving of rights of way, etc. Knowledge of the rules is advantageous for competitors in small boat races.

Racing sails An outfit of special sails carried in addition to a boat's ordinary mainsail and headsail.

Racing tactics Manoeuvres that may help one gain an advantage over another competitor in a race.

Rack, racking A seizing put on parts of a tackle, bollard turns, etc, to bind ropes together and prevent them rendering; it is put on, over, and under each part in a figure of eight, and covered with a number of round turns.

Radar An electronic device for obtaining bearings and distances.

Radio beacon Shore station whose transmissions may be used for direction-finding.

Radio-telephone The short-range telephone service whereby vessels in coastal waters and subscribers ashore may be connected.

Raffee A triangular sail set from the truck of a mast as a skyscraper.

Raft A collection of spars and timbers lashed together to form a floating platform; a buoyant float built for lifesaving.

Rag wagon An old full-rigged ship.

Raise a light Come within view of a light.

Rake The angle of backward inclination of a ship's masts or funnels. The slope of a bow or stern beyond the keel ends.

Ram The projection of a ship's bow at the forefoot.

Ram's head A spiral curved hook to prevent an eye being shaken off.

Randan fashion The method of rowing a boat by three persons: bow and stroke have one oar each, while the third person pulls a pair of sculls in the midship position.

Range The difference between the depth of water at high and low tides.

Range, to To extend, lay out, or place in line, eg a cable for examination. Place cable in the locker to ensure it will run clear when next used. Applied to a vessel when she sheers at anchor.

Rap full Said when all sails are fully stretched by the wind.

Ratcatchers Metal shields fitted around berthing hawsers so that rats may not enter a ship.

Rating The classification of a vessel.

Rating rule A combination of the various qualities of a yacht, from which an index is formed as a rating.

Ratlines The small ropes which cross the shrouds of the rigging to provide steps for going aloft.

Rattle down the rigging To set up the ratlines when they are drooping; to set them all horizontally taut.

Reach A long straight part of a waterway, or a distance between two bends of a river. There may be an upper or lower reach, while that part leading into a harbour is a harbour reach.

Reach, to Sail across the wind, ie with the wind crossing the boat approximately at right-angles to her direction. With the wind just before the beam it is a 'fine reach', on the beam a 'beam reach', and just abaft the beam a 'broad reach'.

Ready about Prepare to go about.

Ready for running Said of a coil of rope that has been capsized after coiling down, or flaked down, so that it will run out freely.

Reamer The gouge used to remove lead pellet remains from a shackle.

Recall A flag or other predetermined signal used to recall boats to a ship or a club house, or to recall men from shore.

Reckon Work out the course on a chart, so that the approximate position may be found.

Red ensign The ensign of the British merchant navy. Any British subject is entitled to fly it in any British ship without formal permission.

Reef Reduce the sail area by folding, rolling, or tying up part of the sails. A chain of rocks lying submerged near the surface.

Reef band A strengthening band of strong canvas sewn across a sail.

Reef becket A becket with a toggle, as used with a reef line (see below).

Reef cringles Thimbles in a leech, to take the reef earings.

Reef earings Short pendants for hauling down and securing the cringle of a reefed sail to a boom.

Reef knot Used to join two ropes together, and made by interlocking the bights formed on each end.

Reef line A rope fixed across a sail, for passing reef beckets; this is a temporary way of reefing or spilling a sail quickly.

Reef points Short lengths of line attached on each side of a sail and spaced out in a row, for tying up the reefed portion.

Reef tackles Used to hook into reef cringles to bowse them to a boom for ease in tying the reef points.

Reefing gear Patent roller fittings used in some small sailing boats, in order to dispense with reef points.

Reeve Pass a rope through any aperture, such as a block, ring, etc.

Refit, refitting A period during which repairs, reconstructions, and replacements are effected (see **Fit out**, p 67).

Regatta A programme of sailing and rowing races, aquatic sports, etc, arranged by an authority or club.

Registered length The measurement from the foremost part of the stem to the after side of the sternpost.

Registered tonnage The net or gross internal capacity of a vessel.

Relieve Place fresh men or ships, called reliefs, on any duty.

Relieving tackles Two purchases rove with one endless fall, placed each side of a large rudder to prevent any undue strain.

Render Assist a rope to move freely and easily. A rope is also said to render if it slips or surges round anything.

Repair on board Return to or join a ship.

Reserve buoyancy Those compartments above water level that may effectively be made watertight.

Restricted class boats A type or group of racing boats of a named length, fixed sail area, and other particular features.

Retire Withdraw from a race.

Reverse laid Rope, for instance, with yarns and strands laid up the same way.

Ribband method The construction of a boat with its planking close-jointed and secured to spaced battens running fore and aft.

Ribs The timbers of a ship or boat, to which planking is secured.

Ride Float secured. A ship is said to 'ride to' or 'ride at' whatever holds her, or to 'ride by' her cable or securing rope. A vessel hove to may 'ride out' a gale, and if making good weather of it, is said to 'ride easily'.

Ride down Be lowered in a bo'sun's chair, as when painting down aloft.

Ride hawse full Pitch, bows under, while at anchor.

Ridge rope A wire rope kept hauled taut in a special position; it has many uses, eg spreading out awnings, life lines, etc.

Riding bitts The bitts to which cable is fastened for riding at anchor.

Riding chocks A bow fitting used as a lead-in for the cable, with a pawl to prevent it running back.

Riding light The anchor light (see p 10).

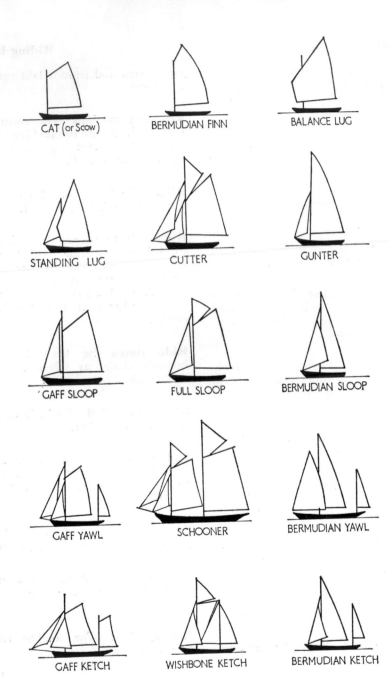

CAT (or Scow)

BERMUDIAN FINN

BALANCE LUG

STANDING LUG

CUTTER

GUNTER

GAFF SLOOP

FULL SLOOP

BERMUDIAN SLOOP

GAFF YAWL

SCHOONER

BERMUDIAN YAWL

GAFF KETCH

WISHBONE KETCH

BERMUDIAN KETCH

Various sailing rigs

Riding scope The length of chain secured by a swivel to the ground scope of moorings laid for small boats; a buoy and buoy-rope are attached to its free end in order to haul it up for use.

Riding slip A spare safety slip fitted in a cable locker, and put on the cable so that the latter may ride by it if anything carries away on deck.

Riding turn That part of a rope taking the strain when it over-rides and jams the preceding turn.

Rig The character, design, and classification of the masts, yards, and sails of a sailing vessel or boat.

Rig, to To set up or fit out, eg to rig a boat for sailing.

Rig the capstan Provide and ship the shoes and bars, and 'pass the swifter', ready for working the capstan by hand.

Rigger One experienced in 'marline-spike seamanship' (see p 113) and rigging work.

Rigging A comprehensive term for all the wires and ropes fitted to stay the masts and work the yards and sails (see **Running rigging** and **Standing rigging**, pp 139 and 155).

Rigging screw A small bottle-screw clamp for tautening shrouds.

Right bank (of a river or stream) The right side when one is looking downstream.

Right of way The legal right of a privileged vessel (see p 128) to hold her course and speed in the vicinity of another.

Right the helm Put it amidships.

Right-handed rope A rope in which the strands form a spiral to the right, as one looks along it. It should be coiled clockwise.

Right-handed screw One whose upper edge turns to starboard seen facing ahead.

Rigol The outboard semi-circular gutterway over a porthole.

Rim-rack Strain and endanger a ship by driving her too hard into a sea.

Ring (of an anchor) The iron hoop to which the cable is secured.

Ring bolt A bolt or plate containing a metal ring to take a block.

Ring stopper A line or chain used to control a large hawser that is being veered; the bight is passed through a ring bolt, to contain the hawser and nip it.

Ringtail A small jib-shaped sail set outside the spanker.

Rip, rip tide A running tide, rising as it flows, and breaking in ripples.

Rise The 'range' (see p 131) of a tide.

Risings The inboard strakes, fore and aft, placed as a support under thwarts.

Roach The concave curve in the foot of a square sail. A curve extending outward of a line, peak to clew, in the leech of a fore-and-aft sail.

Roband, robin, robbin (contractions of 'rope-band') A short line at the head of a square sail to secure it to the jackstay.

Rock the boat Upset the trim of a boat by moving from side to side.

Rockbound Hemmed in by rocks.

Rockered Applied to a keel that is rounded or curved.

Rocket A directional firework used to carry a line or set off as a distress signal.

Rocket apparatus A mobile unit with rocket and line for sending a breeches buoy; stationed round the coast for use when ships are wrecked or grounded close inshore.

Rogue's yarn A small coloured yarn, contrarily twisted, used to distinguish or identify government rope.

Roller A powerful wave that rolls from a deep sea swell.

Rolling Swaying or leaning from side to side, as opposed to pitching.

Rolling hitch Used to tail a small rope to a larger one, and made by taking the first two turns of a clove hitch, jamming them, and bringing the end up through a third turn instead of the second one.

Rooming Running to leeward.

Rooves Small copper washers used when copper nails are clenched.

Rope Cordage of 1in circumference or more, made from yarns of hemp, jute, manila, sisal, coir, etc. Threads of fibre are spun into right-handed yarns that are twisted left-handed into strands, and the strands are laid up right-handed into a right-handed rope.

Rope a sail Sew on the boltrope (see p 25).

Rope yarn Twice-laid yarn, made up from old rope.

Rope yarn knot Used to join two yarns together, by splitting the ends and knotting one part of each together.

Ropemaking The art of spinning, twisting, and laying up of strands to make them into ropes, now done by machines.

Roping needle A large type of sailmaker's needle, with its pointed end curved; used with roping twine for roping sails.

Rotator A brass cone fitted with fins that cause it to rotate when being trailed; it is secured by a 'stray line' to the logline.

Round bilge The curved bulge of a boat's side when not brought out to a chine.

Round down Overhaul a suspended tackle.

Round in Gather in horizontally the slack of a rope.

Round line Small three-stranded stuff, suitable for seizings, etc.

Round seam Join two edges of canvas, one of which is a folded seam.

Round seizing Used to join two parallel parts of rope together; a flat seizing with another layer of turns bound round it.

Round to Bring a ship to the wind. To 'go round' is to tack.

Round turn, bring up with a Stop someone or something abruptly.

Round turn and two half hitches A hitch used to secure a line, eg to the ring of a buoy; it is formed by taking a round turn, bringing the end to the standing part, and taking two half hitches on it.

Round turn, make a Pass a rope in a complete circle round a cleat, pin, or spar, etc.

Round up, to To take in the slack of a rope vertically; to shorten the drift of a tackle when it has been extended after lowering something.

Rounding Small junk or condemned rope, unlaid and used for chafing service. 'Rounding' a point or headland is clearing it in passing.

Roundly Quickly.

Rove Said of a rope when passed through a block or other aperture.

Row Propel a boat by pulling oars.

Rowlock A space in the washstrake, or a crutch fitted into the gunwale, for an oar to rest in when rowing.

Royal A light sail above the topgallantsail for fine weather use. A prefix signifying upper, applied to masts, stays, etc.

Royal Yachting Association The central organisation and national authority for yachtsmen, which ad-

Rubbing strake, rubber

ministers the rules of all national classes and represents the views of the Commonwealth at meetings of the IYRU (International Yacht Racing Union), of which it is a member.

Rubbing strake, rubber A strengthening strip fitted along the sides of a boat outboard of the top strake and secured to the gunwale, as a protective buffer.

Rudder An instrument on the stern of a vessel by which it is steered; a flat frame of wood or metal hinged on the sternpost.

Rudder chains Sometimes fitted each side of a rudder for emergency steering if the rudder head is out of use.

Rudder head The upper end of the rudder which receives the tiller, quadrant, or any other fitting controlled from the wheel.

Rule of the Road *The Regulations for Preventing Collisions at Sea.* A schedule of articles that must be complied with by all vessels on the seas and all navigable waters (see also **Sound signals**, p 152). In addition to the Rules concerning lights (see **Jingles**, p 97) the following Steering Rules are clearly defined to avoid risk of collision:

When two power-driven vessels are approaching each other head on or almost head on, each shall alter

Rule of the road

course to starboard, (ie keep to the right), and pass the other port to port.

When two power-driven vessels are crossing so as to involve a risk of collision, the vessel which has the other on her starboard side shall keep out of the way.

A power-driven vessel overtaking another vessel shall keep out of the way of the vessel being overtaken.

In narrow channels every power-driven vessel shall, when it is safe and practicable, keep to that side of the fairway or channel which lies on the starboard side of that vessel.

When two sailing vessels are approaching one another so as to involve risk of collision, one of them shall keep out of the way of the other, as follows:

A vessel running free shall keep out of the way of a vessel which is close hauled.

A vessel which is close hauled on the port tack shall keep out of the way of a vessel close hauled on the starboard tack.

When both vessels are running free, with the wind on different sides, the vessel which has the wind on her port side shall keep out of the way of the other.

When both vessels are running free, with the wind on the same side, the vessel which is to windward shall keep out of the way.

A vessel with the wind aft shall keep out of the way of the other.

When a power-driven vessel and a sailing vessel are proceeding so as to involve risk of collision, the power-driven vessel shall keep out of the way of the sailing vessel.

ACT PROMPTLY TO AVOID COLLISION AT ALL TIMES.

All vessels should carry a complete copy of these Rules.

All racing competitors should carefully study special racing rules.

Rule of thumb Approximate estimation based on practical experience.

Rumbo Old condemned rope that may be used when strength is not essential, eg for lashings, mats, etc.

Run The distance covered. The after part of a vessel where her lines converge.

Run, to To sail with the wind aft. To travel.

Run out to a clinch With all cable out. With all pockets empty.

Run out to sea A practice adopted by a vessel anchored on a lee shore or in danger from high wind and seas. Run for safety.

Runner and tackle A tackle applied to a runner (see **Tackles**, p 163).

Runners Stays that support a mast when running before the wind.

Running bowline A bowline that

has its standing part running through it as a noose. It should *never* be used round a man's body.

Running fix A method used to fix the ship's position on a chart: a fixed object is selected, and two bearings taken with an interval; the times, course, and distance will enable the 'observed position' (see p 120) to be plotted.

Running free Sailing with wind right aft.

Running knot Made by bighting a rope end and making an overhand knot in the end, containing the standing part; the loop thus forms a noose.

Running part The hauling part of a fall, as distinct from the standing part.

Running rigging All the movable parts of a ship's rigging, as distinct from the shrouds and stays that are permanently set up.

Saddle A wooden chock fixed to a mast or boom for another to rest in.

Safe offing, make a Attain a safe position clear of land.

Safety boards Used in ships with transmitting sets, whereby a board marked 'safe to transmit' can break the main circuit. Anyone going aloft must first obtain this board.

Safety harness Personal buoyancy wear for use in bad weather or when sailing alone, and which can attach the wearer to the boat.

Sag Drift off course. A boat improperly cradled by end supports only is apt to 'sag' in the middle. Opposite to 'hogging'.

Sail Canvas fabric of various sizes and shapes, spread to catch the wind as a means of propulsion. Square sails are bent to yards, and fore-and-aft sails are either bent to a gaff, hanked, or set flying. To sail is to navigate a sailing ship or boat.

Sail cloth A stout canvas fabric of flax and cotton, made up into bolts of canvas. Any one cloth forming part of a sail.

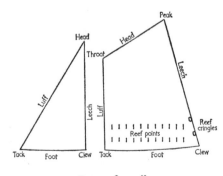

Parts of a sail

Sail close on a wind Keep close with sails full but not shaking.

Sail close to the wind A metaphorical variant of the above; risk being caught, or only just get away with anything.

Sail large Sail with the wind between beam and quarter, and with sheets eased well off; at a larger angle from the wind than close hauled or full and by.

Sail like a haystack Sail badly, making more leeway than headway.

Sail plan A diagram to show a boat's rig and measurements.

Sail track A guideway on a mast in which lugs attached to a luff can travel; used in lieu of hoops or parrel bands.

Sailing A way of plotting a vessel's path and position, eg 'great circle sailing', 'plane sailing', 'middle latitude sailing'.

Sailing committee An elected body of officials who start, control, and interpret the rules of sailing races.

Sailing free Reaching or running, and able to move to either side of the course steered; used in a very different sense from 'running free'.

Sailing thwart A pulling thwart

that can be unshipped to provide more space. A fore-and-aft midship plank secured to the thwarts and used as a support to a mast.

Sailing tiller A special lengthened tiller or yoke fitting, adaptable for better control when sailing (see **Tiller extension**, p 164).

Sailmaker One versed in the art of making sails.

Sailmaker's needle The triangular tapered needle used for canvas work.

Sailmaker's twine or **thread** Special flaxen thread used for working canvas, etc.

Sailmarkings Letters or other insignia sewn on both sides of a sail to show a boat's class and number.

Sailor One who sails in ships; a seaman with practical sailing ability.

Sally Rock a ship in an attempt to free a vessel aground by running the crew from side to side.

Salute A mark of respect, dipping the ensign, letting fly sheets, etc.

Salvage Property recovered from a wreck. Save anything. An equivalent value due to those who salve anything is 'salvage money'.

Salvage hawser The insurance hawser (see p 94).

Sampson post A strong bitt. A kingpost, eg to support a stump derrick.

Sandbank A bank of sand, silt, etc, deposited by the current.

Save-all A drip tin fitted under a scuttle.

Sawn off square With both bow and stern straight up and down.

Saxboard The uppermost strake of an open boat.

Scandalise Spill the wind from a sail; to 'scandalise the mainsail' is to do this by lowering the peak and/or by topping the boom.

Scan the horizon Look all round and as far as the eye can see.

Scantlings Timbers reduced to their structural dimensions.

Scending The upward angular movement of a ship lifted horizontally and bodily by a sea (as distinct from pitching, when bow and stern rise and fall alternately).

Schooner A fore-and-aft-rigged vessel with two or more masts, often called by its rig, eg topsail-, staysail-, gaff-schooner, etc.

Scope Length of any cable or rope paid out, and the space over which it may range; a long length is a 'good scope'.

Score The groove in the shell of a block made to take its strop.

Scotsman, scotchman A wood or metal fitting secured to prevent chafing. Ornamental grating and covering for bollards, etc.

Scow A flat-bottomed boat with broad square ends and straight sides. A shallow tray for hoisting small packages of cargo.

Scowing an anchor A method used to enable a boat's anchor to be tripped; the grapnel is secured to the crown and stopped to the ring.

Screen The vertical surface of any superstructure.

Screw The propeller.

Screw slip stopper A large turnbuckle slip fitted on deck to secure a bower.

Scud Light clouds fleeting along below rain clouds.

Scud, to To run, with studding sails (see p 159) set, before a strong wind.

Scull Propel a boat using two sculls or one oar over the stern.

Sculls Light shortened oars with curved blades.

Scupper, to to sink (see also **Scuttle, to,** below).

Scuppers Holes cut in bulwarks for water to escape overboard from the decks or waterways.

Scuttle, side scuttle A hole through the side for light and air.

Scuttle, to To sink a ship by cutting holes in her or opening inlets.

Sea A large expanse of salt water. A large wave. The swell in a storm.

Sea anchor Timbers and spars lashed together, or any kind of drogue, used as a floating anchor for a vessel to ride to, head to wind, if hove to in bad weather.

Sea breeze A breeze blowing from sea to land, usually just before sunset.

Sea mile A nautical mile (see p 118).

Seaboat The boat kept ready for immediate use at sea. The phrase 'good (or bad) seaboat' describes a craft's adaptability to sea conditions.

Seaborne Carried on the sea.

Seacock A controlling valve fitted to an underwater inlet.

Seam The space between plankings on a deck. One of the two edges of the cloths sewn together in sailmaking.

Seaman One who is conversant with the working of a vessel and has practical knowledge of a ship's equipment, rigging, boats, and all upper deck work. A general term for anyone who works on a ship in any capacity and goes to sea with her.

Seamanlike In a manner that shows good seamanship.

Seamanship The practical art of navigating a vessel or handling a boat. The performing of the many tasks necessary to work a ship, her rigging and boats, etc.

Searoom The sea around a ship clear of obstructions and of the land.

Seaway A deep water channel running in from the sea.

Seaworthy Fit for sea and capable of withstanding adverse weather.

Secure Make fast.

Secure for sea Batten down and lash movable objects, and complete preparations for proceeding to sea.

Seizing A means of binding two parts of rope together to keep them secure; there are various kinds, eg flat, round, etc.

Selvagee A handy strop made from a coil of spunyarn or marline to the size required and tightly marled down.

Semaphore A signalling system by which the extension of the arms in different positions represents letters. Handflags and mechanical arms are sometimes used.

Send down Lower from aloft.

Senhouse A large slip in the cable locker near the clench bolt for holding the cable should it have to be unbolted and slipped.

Sennet, sennit A form of plaited or braided rope made of many strands in various patterns, eg round, flat, English, etc.

Serve Cover the parcelling of a rope or splice neatly with spunyarn or marline to complete the protection. Remember the old jingle:

Worm and parcel with the lay,
Serve the rope the other way.

Serve the cable Bind it with rope, canvas, etc, to keep it from scoring the hawse pipe.

Service Any kind of protective covering wrapped round rope, etc.

Serving board A shaped board used to make a neat serving.

Serving mallet A small mallet grooved to ride a rope when serving.

Set The extent to which a ship leaves her course because of tidal movement.

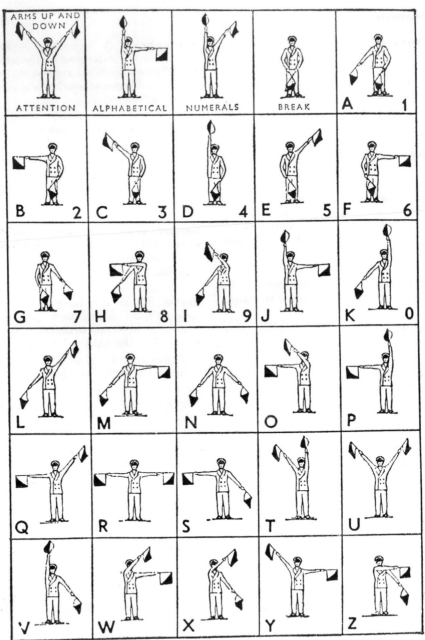

Semaphore code positions

Set, to To place. To hoist or spread a sail ready for trimming.

Set flying Hoisted taut on its own luff and not hanked to a stay, eg a jib.

Set of the tide The direction of a tidal current.

Set sail Spread all sails required in order to proceed.

Set up Tauten in position or ready for use. Position.

Settle Ease gradually and lower slowly. Sink slowly.

Sewed up Pronounced 'sued'. Stranded. A vessel is said to be sewed up a certain distance, to indicate the distance water has dropped below her waterline when aground.

Sextant A navigational instrument for measuring angular distances.

Shackle A metal link, U-shaped and with a bolt; there are many patterns, all used to connect various links and eyes, etc.

Shackle of cable A length of cable 12½ fathoms long. The number of lengths and the size varies with the ship.

Shadow pin A vertical metal pin fixed at the centre of a compass bowl.

Shake Luff so that the sails shake, in order to adjust gear or to enable some defect to be remedied.

Shake a block Dismantle it.

Shake a cask Take it to pieces and bundle up the parts (shakes).

Shake out a reef Let out a reef by casting off (undoing) reef points.

Shakings A collection of old discarded rope, canvas, etc.

Shallows A place over which the water is not deep, eg a shoal.

Shank The long middle part of an anchor; the 'shank painter' is the rope or chain round the shank to secure it to the ship's side.

Shape a course Plan out a proposed route for a vessel.

Sharp at both ends Pointed at bow and stern, double-ended.

Sharp end The bows, as distinct from the blunt end aft.

Sheave The wheel in a block over which a rope is rove.

Sheepshank Used to shorten a rope temporarily without cutting it, or to relieve the strain from any chafed part: a bight is formed in the rope and a half hitch placed over it

K

where required, and the bight remaining is similarly half hitched, the loops formed being seized or toggled if necessary.

Sheer A curve. The fore-and-aft curve of a vessel's deck.

Sheer, to To turn aside. To keep over the tiller of a boat at anchor, so that she moves laterally and avoids fouling her anchor.

Sheer hulk An old ship, unfit for sea, which has been fitted with sheer legs for shipping tall masts into yachts, etc.

Sheer legs, sheers Two or three heavy spars, spread at their heels, to lift heavy weights.

Sheer off Get away; move out or farther off.

Sheer plan The fore-and-aft vertical section plan in boatbuilding.

Sheer poles Iron bars secured horizontally at the foot of a mast's standing rigging to prevent the shrouds turning.

Sheer strake The upper planking on a boat's side; it follows her sheer.

Sheer up alongside Approach at an angle and curve in gradually.

Sheet A rope attached to the clew of a sail and used to trim it.

Sheet anchor A spare anchor. A reserve.

Sheet bend Used to secure one rope to another, or to an eye. Made by passing the end through the bight or eye, round behind it, and back under its own part. The addition of a second turn makes it a double sheet bend.

Sheet clips Metal arms in sailing boats, in which to jam a sheet.

Sheet home Haul the sheet taut.

Shelf A long fore-and-aft timber in yachts, to secure the tops of the timbers and take the beams for the deck. A flat layer of rocks. A sandbank.

Shell (of a block) The case or frame in which the pin is held.

Shifting backstay An additional preventer stay, whose position may be altered to suit certain winds.

Ship A vessel with three masts, and tops and yards fitted to each to spread square sails. Now a general term for any vessel, especially of the large ocean-going types.

Ship, to To receive anything onboard. To put anything in its place.

Ship ahoy The correct nautical hail to a ship.

Ship broker One who buys, sells, or charters for others on commission.

Ship chandler A retailer ashore who specialises in marine supplies.

Ship oars Place them in crutches or rowlocks, ready for use.

Shipboard The deck of a ship.

Shipmate One of a crew.

Shipment The act of putting anything on board. A cargo.

Shipping master One who arranges the engagement of crews, etc.

Ship's company The crew of a ship excluding the officers.

Ship's cousin Anyone who is berthed aft but has to work with the hands.

Ship's husband A person appointed as agent, manager, accountant, etc, by the owners of a vessel.

Ship's master The officer in command of and responsible for a ship.

Ship's papers All documents appertaining to the ship's registry, cargo, clearance, bill of health, etc, that an authority may require.

Shipshape Neat and orderly. Seamanlike.

Shipwreck The loss of a vessel by destruction on a shore, rocks, etc.

Shipwright A shipbuilder, skilled in metal-work.

Shiver Shake the wind out of a sail by luffing. Break in pieces.

Shoal A place where water is shallow and dangerous to navigation.

Shoaling Coming from deeper water to a lesser depth.

Shoe A metal heel fitting, eg for a rudder, capstan bar, etc.

Shoe the anchor Secure planks to its flukes to enable it to bite better in a soft bottom.

Shoot in stays Sail round easily to a new tack without tending to lose way.

Shoot the sun Take its meridional altitude by means of an instrument.

Shoot up Make progress to windward by luffing.

Shore The coast or land adjacent to the sea. A timber or other prop placed in position to act as a support; to 'shore up'.

Shore station A special lookout position on shore established for communication with shipping.

Short boards The frequent tacks needed to beat to windward when sailing in a narrow channel.

Short splice Used to join two rope ends together; the ends are un-laid, butted and married, and each strand is then tucked over and under.

Short stay A taut cable at a smaller angle than 'astay' (see p 12).

Shorten in Take in some of the cable laid out when at anchor.

Shorten sail Reduce the area of sails that are set by taking in, reefing down, or substituting smaller or storm sails.

Shoulder block A block with a squared shaped top to its shell, to prevent its rope binding or jamming against the fixture to which it may be secured.

Shoulder the anchor A boat with insufficient cable to ride by may lift or shoulder her anchor and drift.

Shove off Push off a boat from alongside. Go away.

Shroud plates Chain plates (see p 37).

Shroud-laid Four-stranded, laid round a heart.

Shrouds Wire ropes from a mast-head to the ship's side to support a mast; upper and lower standing rigging.

Side The outer part of a ship between her deck and waterline.

Side lights The red and green navigation lights required by the Rule of the Road, fixed so as to show from right ahead to two points abaft the beam, with red to port and green to starboard and visibility at least 2 miles.

Sight the anchor View it as it breaks surface when being weighed, to see if it is foul or clear.

Sight the land Run in from seaward to take a sight of it.

Sights Observations, angles, etc.

Signal A sign for conveying a message over a distance. Various methods are used, eg flags, sema-phore, Morse, etc, and conveyed by sight, sound, light, etc (see **International code**, p 94).

Signal gun A gun specifically used as a signal, eg for time, starting a race, distress.

Sill The height of a coaming above a deck.

Silt Ooze or other sediment brought into a harbour by the tide and left there. To 'silt up' is to become choked by mounds of silt.

Single anchor, at Riding by one anchor.

Single bend The sheet bend (see p 146).

Single up Cast off all securing hawsers except one at each position.

Single whip A single rope rove through a fixed block (see **Tackles**, p 163).

Single-hander A small yacht that can be managed by one person.

Sinker A weight used with a buoy rope.

Sisal A general purpose rope made from fibres of sisal, a hemp plant.

Sit out Lean out for balance over a weather gunwale on a trapeze in small dinghy sailing.

Skeg, scag The metal socket that supports the base of a rudder.

Skid A timber hung over the side as a protective fender, or used as a roller under a boat to assist moving it along.

Skiff A small light open boat.

Skin The planking or outer covering of a boat. Formerly the inside was the skin and the outside the case.

Skin the bunt, skin a sail Stow a sail by laying the leech along the boom or gaff and rolling the bunt neat and taut. This method is not recommended.

Skipper A seaman who has qualified by examination to act as Master of trawlers and drifters. Often loosely applied to captains of small coastal craft (from the Dutch for sailor).

Skylight A glazed framework built in a deck to admit light and air.

Skysail A small light square sail set above the royal.

Slack The reverse of taut. That part of any rope that is loose.

Slack away, slack off Ease up a rope freely.

Slack in stays Slow and sluggish in going about.

Slack tide or **water** The short interval at the turn of the tide, when there is little current flowing.

Slackness The tendency of a ship to fall from the wind.

Slant A favourable wind. A 'slant tack' is the one most favourable to the course when working to windward.

Slatting The flapping movement of sails swinging idly when wind fails.

Sleepers Knees that connect the transom to the after timbers.

Slew Turn; turn anything about its axis.

Sliding thwarts Special movable thwarts fitted to facilitate rowing in boats built for racing.

Sliding ways Fitments attached to a vessel for moving over the ground ways of a slip at the launching.

Sling A rope or chain passed to anything for hoisting. A large rope strop. 'To sling' is to prepare anything for hoisting by using a sling.

Sling your hook Move off.

Slip A metal stopper with a tongued eye; the tongue is passed through the eye of a rope or around the cable and brought back within a small retaining link. A quick release is obtained by knocking off the link (see also **Slipway**, below).

Slip, to To knock off a slip. To drop a seaboat by releasing the disengaging gear. To let go a mooring chain. To 'slip a cable' is to let it all go without weighing the anchor. To

lose touch with the way of doing things.

Slip by the board Slide down the ship's side.

Slip knot, slippery hitch A knot, bend, or hitch that will give when strain comes upon it.

Slip rope A wire rove through the ring of a buoy and brought to a slip onboard while the bridles are unshackled and anchors stowed. A rope used as a temporary hold, to be slipped when required.

Slipway, slip A dock, hard, or way with a sloping surface extending to the water, over which vessels may be hauled up or launched.

Sloop A sailing vessel with one mast, fixed bowsprit, and jib stay; under full sail sloops wear mainsail, foresail, topsail, and jib. Various rigs are called sloops, but the gradual disappearance of bowsprits and topsails has changed the description 'sloop-rigged' to signify a vessel with one mast and two sails (mainsail and jib).

Slope an awning Bowse alternate earings to the deck in wet weather.

Slow marks Two leading marks so close together that when they are seen in line from a boat, they do not 'open' until the boat has moved some distance.

Smack A partly decked boat used for trawling. The term is now generally applied to all fishing vessels that sail.

Small stuff Collective term for spunyarn, marline, other small lines and yarns.

Snag A submerged obstacle (hence the term 'hitting a snag').

Snarled Kinked or tangled.

Snatch An open lead used to direct a rope; if there is no roller or sheave, it is a 'dumb snatch'.

Snatch a rope Lay the bight over the sheave of a snatch block and close the hinge, the block being placed to give a lead.

Snatch a turn Take a quick turn on a bollard, cleat, or anything handy.

Snatch block A block with a hinged side opening to take the bight of a rope without one having to reeve it all.

Sneer Strain a ship when sailing by using too much canvas.

Snots A ship's bows.

Snotter The lower support to a sprit. A rope loop used to prevent anything to which it is attached from slipping.

Snow A brig with an auxiliary mast abaft her mainmast, on which a fore-and-aft gaff sail is used.

Snub Suddenly check anything running out.

Snubbing Said of a boat jerking at her anchor at short stay.

Snug Lying comfortably in a place of shelter. Stowed neatly away. Secured.

Snug down Reduce, take in, and be under proper sail to meet a gale.

Sny The upward curvature of a plank. The toggle used with a flag.

Soft eye An eye splice not fitted with a thimble.

Soft iron correctors Two balls, usually of soft Swedish iron, placed near a compass to correct the magnetism induced by the iron in a ship.

Soldier's wind A 'fair wind' (see p 64).

Sole piece A timber foot fitted to the heel of a rudder, so that it will easily detach should a boat take the ground.

Sound A narrow channel or passage of water.

Sound, to To ascertain the depth of water.

Sound signals A group of signals made in accordance with the Rule of the Road by siren, foghorn, etc, between vessels *in sight of each other* to communicate messages. One short blast indicates 'I am altering course to starboard'; two short blasts, 'I am altering course to port'; while three short blasts signify 'My engines are going full speed astern'. Other important messages are signalled by a single letter which conveys a meaning similar to its International Code Flag meaning (see p 95). There is a separate group of signals for use in fog (see p 71) when ships are not in sight.

Sounding machine A machine containing a reel of fine piano wire to which a chemically treated tube is attached near the 'dipsey'; it is used for sounding deep water without stopping the ship (see also **Boxwood scale**, p 27).

Sounding pipe A pipe led down through a ship to the well, in which a 'sounding rod' is used to sound the depth of water.

South A cardinal point; the direction of the sun at noon.

South-east The point midway between south and east.

South-west The point midway between south and west.

South-wester, sou'wester A painted canvas hat with a broad flap, as worn with oilskins.

Southing The distance made good towards the south.

Spanish reef A figure of eight knot in the head of a sail.

Spanker The gaff-rigged sail set on a mizzen-mast, sometimes called the 'driver'.

Spanking Sailing with a strongish wind with the spanker boomed out to good effect. It also implies force, eg a spanking wind.

Spar A general term for any mast, yard, gaff, boom, pole, etc.

Spar buoy A buoy of which only a spar is visible when in position.

Speak a vessel Pass within hail of another ship to establish vocal communication. Communicate by signal, whether in sight or not (see also **Gamming**, p 77).

Spell A fixed period of time, such as that taken up by a special duty, or the rest period between 'tricks'.

Spencer A loose-fitted sail set abaft a mast with its head extended.

Spherical buoy A dome-topped buoy with horizontal bands, used to mark the middle ground (see p 114) or an isolated danger.

Spider band, hoop An iron band around a mast, derrick, or spar, fitted with eyes to take the shackles of shrouds, guys, etc; on a mast it may also carry belaying pins for the running gear.

Spilling the wind, spillage Any method used to make a sail ineffective by causing it to lose its wind.

Spin a yarn, dit, dippy, twist, bender, cuffer, fairy-tale Tell a long-drawn-out story, welcome on a long dreary watch. The proverbial 'pinch of salt' is often necessary.

Spindrift Spray whipped off and blown from the crests of waves.

Spinnaker A large balloon-shaped jib set on the opposite side to the mainsail when running; if cut full, it has two leeches and clews.

Spinnaker boom A spar to spread the foot of a spinnaker, sometimes called a spreader; it should be fitted with a downhaul in large boats.

Spinnaker topsail An additional topsail set on a short boom.

Spirketting Deck planks that fit over the beam ends.

Spit A projecting sandbank that runs out from a point.

Spitfire The small storm jib, specially made of strong canvas.

Splash boards Portable strakes fitted on to the gunwales of boats when sailing.

Splay tackle A tackle used between heels of sheer legs to maintain them in position.

Splice Join two parts of rope together by unlaying the strands and interweaving them; different methods are employed according to the purpose (see **Short, Long, Back,** and **Cut splice**, pp 148, 108, 13 and 50).

Split tacks Applied to two vessels beating to windward, when they separate from each other and proceed on different tacks.

Spoil ground A charted area set apart for depositing dredgings.

Sponson A permanent platform erected on the outside of a ship.

Spray Particles of water blown from the surface of the sea.

Spring A hawser secured amidships and used, when a ship is 'tied up' alongside, to prevent her from surging back and forth. There are 'fore springs' led forward to the jetty, and 'back springs' led aft. Either may be used to 'spring her off' when she leaves, ie to retain bow or stern at the jetty while working the other end away by use of engines and wind or tide.

Spring a leak Spring a plank that begins to let water in.

Spring hook One with a spring catch closing its bill as a retainer.

Spring ship Point a ship in any required direction; a hawser is passed outboard from the quarter and secured to the cable, so that, by veering the cable, the ship will gradually turn off at an angle.

Spring tides Those tides at which the range between high and low water is greatest, and which occur just after a full or new moon, when sun, earth, and moon are somewhat in line.

Sprit A boom set diagonally across a sail from the mast up to the peak.

Sprit sail A fore-and-aft sail supported and extended by a sprit.

Sprung Said of any mast or spar that is damaged by strain and may be unsafe.

Spunyarn A coarse thick yarn made of twisted marline, tarred, and supplied in pads; used for servings and small lashings.

Spurnwater A beading or coam-

ing fitted to prevent water spilling over.

Squall A brief but sudden gust of high wind; sometimes called black or white, according to whether or not dark clouds prevail.

Square knot The reef knot.

Square lashing The 'over and under' lashing passed alternately round two spars to bind them together at right-angles to each other.

Square rig A ship with square sails set crosswise, as distinct from fore-and-aft sails in a fore-and-aft line; loosely applied to a ship that sets any square sails.

Square sail A four-sided sail extended by a yard at right-angles to a mast.

Stabiliser A fitting intended as a non-roll unit.

Staff A light pole set up to carry the ensign or jack, or a topmark on a buoy.

Stage A plank suspended by a rope at each end, for men to sit or stand on when working over the side.

Stage lashing Soft rope specially supplied for lashings and stage lanyards, and unsuitable for great strain.

Staghorn   A metal bollard with two horizontal arms.

Stanchion   A fixed upright pillar support of iron or wood, between decks, or for guard rails, awnings, etc.

Stand   Steer in a certain direction.

Stand by   Remain close to a vessel that may need assistance. Be prepared and ready to act.

Stand in   Approach.

Stand of tide   A prolonged period of high water; a 'double tide' (see p 57).

Stand off   Keep away; wait clear of any position.

Stand on   Maintain one's course and speed.

Standard compass   The large magnetic compass on the bridge, situated with an all-round view for taking bearings.

Standard port   A port included in the many published lists that show the predicted times and heights of high and low water.

Standing main   A fore-and-aft mainsail, as used in a dipping lug

cutter; the foot is bent to a boom, which can be topped by the 'main boom topping lift' when wearing.

Standing part   The main or original part of anything, without addition or before it was altered. That part of a sheet or tackle that is made fast, as distinct from the hauling part.

Standing rigging   Those parts of the rigging such as shrouds, stays, etc, that may be set up permanently.

Standing topping lift   A wire span to suspend a derrick not in use.

Starboard   The right-hand side of a ship looking forward from inboard, opposite to port.

Starboard tack   Sailing with the wind on the starboard side.

Starboard the helm   Put the tiller to starboard.

Starboard the wheel (usually **Starboard** 10, or another number)   Put the wheel (with rudder and ship's head) to starboard to the number of degrees indicated.

Starboard watch   The opposite watch to the port watch (see p 128).

Starboard-hand buoys   Those that mark the right-hand side of a channel seen from the entrance to harbour, or going with the main stream of a flood tide (see **Conical buoys**, p 47).

Start   The firing of a gun or lowering of both flags indicate the start of a sailing race. Should the gun misfire, the lowering of the flags is the actual time of the start.

Starting   In sailing races a yacht is deemed to have started when any part of her, or her crew, crosses the starting line in the direction of the first mark; if too soon, she must return clear behind the line and restart. Said of any wooden fitting showing signs of loosening or breaking.

Starved   A vessel is 'starved' when sailed too close to the wind.

Stations   The consecutive numbers of a ship's frames.

Staunched   Watertight.

Stave off   Push and keep away, using a stave or pole.

Stayband   An iron hoop encircling a mast with eyes to take the stays.

Stays   That part of the standing rigging supporting the masts in a fore-and-aft direction and extending from the masthead forward and

downward. They remain as set up, and are named from the mast they support.

Staysail   A triangular sail extended on a stay, and named from that stay, eg forestaysail. In one-masted boats the foresail, or inner of two, is termed a staysail if hanked to the stay.

Steady   A helm order to keep the ship on a course given.

Stealer   A short plank in the strakes.

Steamer, steamship   Every mechanically propelled vessel is a steamer for Rule of the Road purposes.

Steaming light   The white masthead light carried on the foremast to denote that a vessel is a steamship; an 'additional steaming light' is carried on the mainmast of large vessels at least 15ft higher than the foremost one. Each shall be visible for 5 miles, and show an unbroken light over an arc of 20 points, ie from right ahead to two points abaft the beam each side.

Steer   Direct the course of a ship by the use of wheel or tiller.

Steerage way   Movement through the water fast enough to enable a boat to be steered effectively.

156

Stem, stempiece The timber at the bow of a ship into which the planks are butted.

Stem the tide Make way against the tide.

Stemson A curved timber behind the apron to support the stem.

Step A wooden hollow, or metal frame, fixed on the keelson, into which the foot of a mast is stepped.

Stepped hull A type of planing hull with surfaces at different levels.

Stern The after part of a ship or boat.

Stern on With the stern directed towards anything, such as the seas that follow the boat.

Stern sheets The space and benches at the after end of a boat.

Sternboard A vessel 'falling back' (going backwards) owing to wind or tide is said to 'make a sternboard'.

Stern-fast A rope used for making fast to anything and led out from aft.

Sternpost The after vertical timber to which the rudder is secured.

Sternway The movement of a vessel propelled stern first.

Stiff Not easily heeled over, even with all sails set; the opposite to 'cranky'.

Stirrup The rope supports from a yard to carry the footropes.

Stock The bar or cross-beam through the upper part of the shank of a 'stocked anchor'; it is set at right-angles to the arms.

Stockless anchor An anchor that has no stock, so that it may be stowed in a hawse pipe.

Stocks A pattern of blocks and shores on which a vessel is built.

Stop up Pass a series of stops (small yarns) round a rope ranged to run out, or round a sail, so that they may be released or carried away in turn. Secure anything back out of the way by means of stops.

Stopper A short rope, chain, or fitting used to hold another rope or chain temporarily. To 'pass a stopper', secure one end, eg to an eyebolt, make the first part of a rolling hitch, and dog the end, either held or seized back, along the lay; with a rope stopper dog with the lay, but with a chain stopper dog against the lay.

Stopper knot A knot used to end off a rope; it is made like a wall knot but with the ends passed on through their next loops before being brought up to be whipped together.

Stopwater Material plugged in the planking to stop a leak.

Storm A commotion of the atmosphere producing strong winds and rain.

Storm cone, storm signal A black cone, 3ft high and 3ft wide at its base, hoisted by shore stations as a warning; if the point is upwards the storm is expected from the north, if inverted, from the south.

Storm jib The spitfire (see p 153).

Storm sail A stout sail of reduced size for use in stormy weather; there are two types, the storm jib and trysail.

Stormbound Delayed or unable to proceed because of a storm.

Stove in Damaged by anything breaking through into a ship (see **Bilged**, p 21).

Stow Put a thing in its allotted place; to find a place for a thing and put it there, the place being termed its 'stowage'.

158

Strait A narrow passage between two oceans or seas.

Strake The full length of one breadth of a boat's planking from stem to stern.

Strand Several rope yarns twisted together to make a part ready to lay up to form a rope. That part of a beach covered and uncovered by tides.

Stranded Run ashore. Helpless and abandoned.

Stray line The line secured to a rotator, attaching it to the logline. When using a logchip (see p 108), it is that part between the turnmark (see p 168) and log.

Stream a buoy Put it into the water, first taking it aft and floating it clear, so as not to foul anything.

Stream anchor An anchor smaller than a bower but larger than a kedge.

Stretch To sail a long way without tacking is to make a long 'stretch' or board.

Stretchers Stout battens in the bottom of pulling boats, placed athwartships, for oarsmen to use with their feet. Spreaders.

Stretching a sail All new sails,

especially if used for racing, should be bent on hand taut without strain, first used in light winds, and gradually weathered to take up their proper shape.

Strike   Lower anything (the word 'down' being superfluous), eg strike topmast, strike a flag, etc.

Strike soundings   Obtain a bottom when approaching land from deep water.

Stringers   In ship construction all small fore-and-aft subsidiary girders, planking, shelving, etc, connected to and supported by a main structure, as a strong internal fastening.

Strip to a gantline   Unrig all rigging except one rope attached to the masthead.

Stroke   The sweep of an oar; it may be timed, and described as being quick, long, or short; the 'stroke oar' is the aftermost one, or the starboard after one in double-banked boats, with which the others keep stroke (time). He sets the time of the stroke.

Strongback   A strong portable timber, placed across a boat to support a heavy anchor slung under it to be laid out, or fitted up to take a towing bollard, etc.

Strop   A ring of rope fitted round a block or spar, often with a thimble

seized in it, to take a shackle. A large ring of rope used to sling a hoist.

Studding sail, stunsail   A narrow sail used in light winds, set at the outer edges of square sails to extend the sail area.

Substitute   One of the special flags used in lieu of another, to avoid carrying more than one set of flags.

Sugging   Rocked by the motion of the sea when stranded.

Surf   The crests of waves that roll in to shallows and break on a foreshore.

Surfing   Utilising the crest of a wave to plane along.

Surge   Suddenly yield and slacken a rope brought to a capstan, winch, etc, when the strain becomes excessive. Permit the cable to run out by its own weight.

Survey   An examination of a vessel, or part of her, or of her stores. Observations and information collated for hydrographical use.

Swab   A mop for drying decks, made from strands of old rope.

Swab hitch   The familiar old term for 'sheet bend'.

Swallow The space between the sheave and shell of a block through which a rope is rove.

Swash A shoal or bank in a tideway that does not uncover but over which the water will ripple or surge at low water.

Swashway A navigable channel through a swash.

Sweep A long oar. A wire towed between two vessels sweeping.

Sweeping The systematic dragging of an area by two vessels using a sweep.

Swell A long continuous succession of rollers that do not break until they meet an obstruction.

Swift a ship or **boat** Pass strong under-girdles around a ship or boat, outside all, to keep her from straining.

Swifter A long line used to retain capstan bars in position when they are shipped. It is middled by a cut splice. To 'pass a swifter', put the cut splice on one bar and take the two ends to the neighbouring bars; lift each bar as the rope is passed over it and back hitched; the bars are thus equally spaced, with an upward cant for breasting.

Swig, sweat To swig or sweat-up

160

on a rope is to take half a turn with one hand while heaving and taking up the slack with the other.

Swing A vessel secured to a buoy, or at anchor, is said to swing as she moves to changing winds or tides.

Swing compasses, swing ship Turn a ship through the compass to point on various bearings, for ascertaining deviation or for calibrations, etc.

Swing the lead Heave the lead by under-arm swinging only, instead of over-arm above one's head (thus doing anything the easy way, or spinning a job out).

Swivel block One so fitted that its eye or hook will turn.

Swivel link One so made that it will turn on a self-contained axis; it is fitted in a cable to keep out the turns.

Sword matting Chafing material made of any number of strands, each passed alternately up and down over successive passings of a cross weft line.

Tabernacle An upright supporting frame to house the foot of a mast.

Tabling The strengthened hem of

a sail to which a boltrope is sewn. The angling piece sewn at the clew and tack.

Tack The lower fore corner of a sail by which it is kept amidships.

Tack, to To go about, from one board to the other, through the wind. A vessel is said to be on the port or starboard tack according to the side the wind is coming over. 'Tacking' is opposite to 'wearing'.

Tack line A 6ft length of signal halyard, used to separate groups of flags in the same hoist.

Tack tackle The tackle used for hauling down the tack of a sail.

Tacking down wind A safety method used when running with a strong wind that may make gybing dangerous; the vessel is brought round to the wind, put about, and the sheets eased as she pays off.

Tackle A purchase formed by the use of rope and blocks; there are many combinations, but those in general use are illustrated (p 163).

Taff rail A rail (usually a hand rail) on the counter of a vessel; the stern rail.

Tail A rope spliced or fitted to a block so that it may be fixed in any required position.

Take Ascertain, by observation or calculation, eg bearings, etc.

Take a turn Pass a rope round a cleat once or twice to take the strain.

Take charge Become uncontrollable.

Take in Furl, brail, or lower and manhandle a sail to gather it in.

Take the strain or **weight** Man a rope and hold the strain, so that turns may be taken.

Take up A boat's planking is said to 'take up' as it swells and becomes staunched to stop any leaks.

Take up (or **down**) **the slack** Gather and pull a rope straight, ready for use.

Taking off Refers to tides when they decrease daily, ie during the period from springs to neaps.

Tall ship A square-rigged ship fitted with topmasts.

Tarpaulin Weatherproof protective cloth made of hemp, jute, linen, etc, treated with a tar-like preparation.

Taunt With very high masts.

L

Taut Stretched out tight or straight. In good condition.

Taut leech The sign of a sail well set and trimmed full.

Telemotor A mechanical apparatus that transmits the turning of the wheel to the steering engine.

Telescope An optical instrument with sliding parts, used to view distant objects.

Tempest A violent wind-storm accompanied by rain.

Templates Wooden pattern moulds from which a boat is shaped.

Tend Attend to the working of.

Tender A small vessel that attends a larger one. A vessel that inclines to heel over well to any moderate winds.

Ten-fathom line A chart marking shown as a succession of dots and dashes along which there is a uniform depth.

Territorial waters The sea adjacent to a country's coastline.

Thames measurements (TM) A method adopted for calculating the tonnage of yachts, based on the length on deck and extreme breadth.

Thief's knot Formed to appear as a reef knot, being interlocked with ends set on opposite sides to show if tampered with.

Thimble A concave grooved metal eye, round or heart-shaped, around which a rope is nipped and spliced to make a hard eye.

Thin end The bows of a vessel, as distinct from the thick end aft.

Tholes, thole pins Wooden pegs shipped vertically in the gunwale and used to contain an oar; now superseded by crutches.

Thrashing to windward Beating up in rough weather.

Threefold purchase A purchase rove through two treble blocks.

Three-letter points The eight intermediate points, each named by three letters—NNE, ENE, ESE, SSE, SSW, WSW, WNW, and NNW.

Throat The upper fore corner of a fore-and-aft sail.

Throat seizing The seizing confining the thimble within the strop of a block and bedding the strop in the score.

Thrum mat A piece of canvas or other coarse material into which

FOR HOISTING

Common
single whip

Two methods
double whip

Luff
(or Watch tackle)

Twofold
purchase

Single and double (Spanish) burton

FOR HAULING

Luff upon luff

Gun tackle

Runner

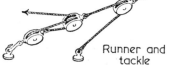

Runner and
tackle

Tackles, etc, in general use

thrums are inserted, either roughly for chafing purposes and collision mats, or decoratively with materials suitable for homes.

Thrums   Small cuttings of strands or other material for making mats.

Thumb cleat   A small cleat of one arm, fixed to a spar, and useful for jamming or holding a rope.

Thumb knot   The overhand knot.

Thummel   The sailmaker's palm (see **Palm**, p 123).

Thwarts   The seats placed athwartships on which oarsmen sit.

Tidal basin   A partly enclosed dock area, open and subjected to any tide level.

Tidal harbour   A harbour to which entrance is possible only at some time during the flood.

Tidal wave   An exceptionally large wave caused by some phenomenon, such as an earthquake, etc.

Tide   The continual rise and fall of the ocean waters.

Tiderode   Riding to the force or with the run of the tide.

Tideway   The main passage of a stream where the tide runs strongest.

Tiers, Tyers   Canvas bands or short ropes for securing sails when furled.

Tiller   A wood or metal bar shipped in a rudder head to steer a boat.

Tiller extension   An additional folding length fitted to a tiller for use in sailing.

Timber   Large pieces of wood, as used in shipbuilding.

Timber hitch   A hitch specially useful for 'log towing' (see p 108); the rope is passed round the spar, round its own standing part, and two or three times back round its own part.

Timberheads   Heads of vertical timbers that rise above deck level.

Timbers   The ribs of a wooden vessel.

Tingle   A patch placed over a hole or leak in a hull.

Toe straps   Webbing or canvas bands secured to stretchers or the bottom of a boat for use as footholds when rowing or sitting out (see **Sit out**, p 149).

Toggle　A short piece of hard wood, tapered at its ends and scored around its centre, to insert in a rope, or act as a stopper.

Tonnage　A term used to describe the size of a vessel: 'gross tonnage' relates to the total interior space, measured cubically, and 'net tonnage' to the cargo-carrying capacity. 'Displacement' is actual weight.

Top　A platform at the head of a mast to extend topmast shrouds; formerly a fighting position, and named from its mast.

Top, to　To raise one end of a derrick or boom by means of a topping lift.

Top hamper　All gear and fittings on and above the upper deck of a small yacht. A hindrance to stability or an obstacle.

Topgallantmast　The third mast above the deck.

Topgallantsail　The sail set above the topsail.

Topmarks　Distinguishing marks placed atop the staffs of buoys, beacons, etc.

Topping lift　The tackle or rope used for supporting and raising any derrick or boom over a hoist.

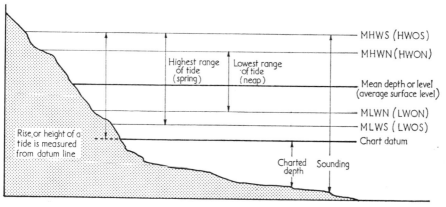

Tidal changes

HW	high water	N	neaps
LW	low water	O	ordinary
M	mean	S	springs

Note carefully the information at or near the chart heading regarding the chart datum and whether soundings are in fathoms or feet, or in metric measurements

Topsail A sail that is set over a mainsail; in square-rigged ships it is the sail next above the course.

Topsail schooner A schooner with square sails on the foremast only (see also **Double topsail schooner**, p 57).

Topsides Freeboard. The bulwarks. That part of a vessel's side out of the water. Literally, the top of the sides.

Topstrake The upper strake of a boat, secured to the gunwale.

Toss your oars In double-banked boats the order to lift the oars to a vertical position, blades fore and aft, as when coming alongside; to 'toss and boat oars' is to toss them, turn inboard, and lay them down amidships, blades forward.

Tousing, towsing A severe beating inflicted by weather or otherwise.

Tow Picked oakum. Anything being towed is referred to as 'the tow'.

Tow, to To pull another vessel through the water by a rope or cable attached to a vessel.

Towing bollard A special portable post which may be shipped into a pre-strengthened fitting, and by which a boat may be towed by another.

Towing bridle A catenary (see p 36).

Towing thwart The foremost thwart in a boat, when made to receive a portable towing bollard.

Towrope, towline A hawser suitable for taking another vessel in tow.

Track The line of course. A ship's wake.

Trail boards Decorative boards adorning a ship's side near the stern.

Trail oars Permit the oars to swing in the rowlocks with the blades trailing aft.

Trailing Towing a boat on a trailer behind a car, ie from the boathouse in a garden to the water's edge.

Trailing edge The leech of a fore-and-aft mainsail with no boltrope.

Transom The piece bolted to the sternpost to extend athwartships across the stern; it shapes the buttocks and holds the planking.

Transom knee The knee angling the hog and sternpost.

Transom stern   A flat stern.

Trapeze   In sailing dinghies a sliding support used by the crew for outboard balancing when they lay up to windward.

Trapping line   A line passed round a towrope, from a ship's quarter, to keep it clear of the propeller if the tow parts.

Traveller   A metal ring or fitting that may be sent or hauled out along a boom, or up and down a mast.

Traverse   To resolve a traverse is to reduce various courses consecutively made by a ship to one course and distance.

Treenail   A bolt made of hard wood, used to secure timbers, planks, etc.

Trestle-trees   The fore-and-aft supports for the top at a masthead.

Triangular course   A sailing race plan with three legs; it usually includes a long beat, a reach, and a run down wind.

Triatic stay   A horizontal stay between masts, for hoisting windsails, flags, etc.

Trice   Lift or haul up something out of the way by means of a 'tricing line'.

Trick   Any one of the various duties of the watch on deck, eg helmsman, lookout, etc, allocated in one- or two-hour 'tricks'.

Trick wheel   The after auxiliary steering wheel at the rudder head.

Tricoloured lantern   The red, white, and green lantern used on the foremast by steam trawlers; it shows over 8, 4, 8 points respectively.

Trigger   Release, eg the dogshore forming the final obstruction when launching a ship, or a close stowing anchor.

Trim   The difference in draught between forward and aft. The set of a vessel on the water. The set of a sail used to best advantage. Neat.

Trim the dish   Sit in a boat so that she does not list.

Trimaran   A boat with three hulls positioned abreast and joined together by beams; sails well but still in the experimental stage.

Trip hook   A hook with an additional eye fitted for attaching a 'trip wire', which, when secured, will trip the hook and release the hoist as it is lowered for the 'tripping line' to take the weight.

Trip the anchor   Break it out of the ground.

167

Trot A system of buoys laid out in line.

Truck A circular piece of wood used as a cap to a mast; it protects the end grain and is usually fitted with sheaves for flag halyards.

Trunnion hoop A hinged hoop fitted to the cap of a mast to contain the mast next above it.

Trysail A reduced sail used instead of a mainsail during a storm.

Tug A powerful vessel specially constructed for the towing of others.

Tumble home The inclination inboard of the upper part of a ship's side.

Turk's head An ornamental knot, so called from its resemblance to a turban.

Turn To 'catch' or 'take a turn' is to pass a rope round a bollard, cleat, or belaying pin, to hold it.

Turn for lowering Take off the surplus turns of a belayed rope, and back up sufficient remaining turns to render it round.

Turn in Swing a davit inboard after anything is hoisted on it; a boat and its davits are then said to be 'turned in'.

Turn of the bilge, or **hull** The curvature where the bottom and side of a vessel meet.

Turn of the tide That period of slack water during the change from flood to ebb (and vice versa).

Turn up To turn up is to belay a rope, putting on sufficient turns for it to be left unattended.

Turning room The amount of space available or required to turn a ship in.

Turnmark The mark on the logline used with a logship, which, as it passes over the quarter, is used as the signal to turn the log glass and begin counting the knots.

Turtle A bag to contain a spinnaker ready for use.

Twin screw A vessel with two propellers on separate shafts.

Two blocks A term denoting that the two blocks of a purchase are drawn as close together as possible; also termed 'choc-a-block'.

Twofold purchase A purchase which has its rope rove through two double blocks (see **Tackles**, p 163).

Tyers See **Tiers**, p 164.

Unbend

Unbend Undo a bend or lacing. Cast loose a sail from its boom or gaff.

Unbitt Take the turns of cable off the bitts.

Unbroken light A Rule of the Road definition of a light showing, unobstructed, over the prescribed arc of visibility.

Under bare poles With no sails set.

Under canvas, under sail In motion and propelled only by the force of wind acting on the sails.

Under the lee Sheltered from the wind by land or an object.

Under the weather Said of any person unwell; out of sorts.

Under way Moving through the water. Any vessel not at anchor, or secured to another, and not aground or made fast to anything ashore, is considered as being under way.

Undercurrent A current under the surface of the water. Any influence at work that is not apparent on the surface.

Underfoot Under the ship's bottom. An anchor is carried underfoot

when lowered and carried short of the bottom, and dropped underfoot when dropped straight down, as a second anchor would be when the main anchor continues to drag.

Undermanned Short-handed; carrying insufficient crew.

Under-run Work back along accessible rope to recover or clear anything, or to haul a boat along a line in the water.

Undertow An undercurrent running in a different direction to that of the water above it. The backwash of water, as in a receding breaker. A strong 'counter current' (see p 47).

Underwriter One who insures ships and their cargoes against loss or damage.

Uniform system of buoyage The Trinity House system used in British coastal waters. It is at variance with that used in some countries, and yachtsmen visiting other waters should first study any differences.

Union hook A special cargo hook that may be attached to two separate whips.

Union Jack, union flag The British national flag; flown on the jack-staff of naval ships. No merchant ship is permitted to use it.

169

Unmoor

Unmoor Weigh and hoist one anchor (removing the mooring swivel, if used), so that a ship remains riding at single anchor.

Unreeve Pull a rope out from any block or sheave.

Unrig Dismantle; strip.

Unship Remove anything from its place of use.

Unwritten law of the sea Never to pass by any ship or boat in distress, but to stand by her and to render whatever assistance may be possible.

Up and down Said of the cable when the ship is brought over her anchor.

Up topsides The hail to someone on the upper deck from someone working over the side, or in a boat alongside.

Upper deck The highest deck that is constructed to extend continuously from stem to stern.

Upperworks All superstructures of a vessel above her upper deck.

Uptake A shaft or pipe to ventilate a compartment.

Vulgar establishment

Van The foremost ships in a fleet; 'in the van' means leading.

Vane A weathercock.

Vang A rope used to keep the peak of a gaff or sprit from sagging to leeward.

Variation The angle between true North and magnetic North; it varies in different parts of the world, and may be either easterly or westerly.

Veer Pay out a rope or cable. Change direction as does the wind.

Very's lights A pyrotechnic signal of either red, white, or green stars, made in a cartridge fired by a Very's pistol.

Vessel Any ship navigated at sea or in coastal waters, excluding small craft and 'boats'.

Visible horizon The circle bounding the view of an observer.

Voyage A journey by water to a distant place, also referred to as a 'passage' or 'trip'.

Vraic, wrack Seaweed.

Vulgar establishment A port establishment (see p 127); the time interval between transit of the moon at 'full and change' and the next high water.

Waist The middle part of a ship's upper deck, usually between the fore and after hatches, or abaft the foremast to the midship part.

Wake The disturbed pattern of water left in the track of a vessel under way; often useful as a guide to observe leeway. A vessel is said to be in the wake of another when she follows in her track.

Wale The thickest strakes along a ship's side, just above the waterline.

Walk away An order to step out smartly with a hawser, etc.

Walk back A method used to lower or ease out a rope, whereby it is kept in hand instead of round a bollard or cleat.

Wall a rope Form a wall knot along, or on the end of, a rope.

Wall knot A knot used as a collar or stopper on a rope; as the ends come out at the top, the rope may be laid up again or whipped and cut. It is frequently used with a crown knot to enlarge it, and may shape as a wall and crown or crown and wall.

Wall-sided Having perpendicular sides.

Wandering Needing to carry rudder or helm to keep a vessel steady.

Ware A variant of 'wear' (see below).

Warm the bell Act before the appropriate time. Steal time.

Warp Move a ship to or from a berth by means of ropes (warps).

Warps Ropes used for moving a ship; towropes.

Wash The turbulent water left behind by any vessel.

Wash down Scrub and wash the upper deck. When seas come inboard over the decks, the vessel is said to be 'washing down'.

Watch For the purpose of working a ship, the hands are normally divided into two watches, called port and starboard. The watch on duty is called the 'watch on deck', the other is the 'watch below'. A watch is also a division of time, normally of 4 hours (see also **Dog watches**, p 56).

Watch tackle The alternative name for a luff (see **Tackles**, p 163).

Watch there, watch Warning

used when working a hand deep-sea line; hands are stationed along the side, each with a coil, and on releasing the last turn, each calls to the man abaft him.

Watching A buoy is watching when it is floating.

Water ballast Water carried to stabilise an empty ship, it being pumped out as cargo is loaded.

Waterborne A ship sustained or lifted by the sea is waterborne, as are goods transported by sea or river.

Waterlaid rope Cable-laid rope (see **Cable laid**, p 33).

Waterline The top edge of the boot-topping, or bottom colour paint, where it meets the topside colour. The line to which water rises.

Watermarks The fore and after set of figures denoting draught marks. Oil and other marks above the waterline that spoil the appearance of the ship's side.

Watertight doors and hatches Those fitted into bulkheads and decks of compartments, which may be easily and quickly closed and clipped to render the partition wateright.

Waterways The deck drainage

space and gully along the upper deck on each side, close to the ship's side.

Wave A surge of water, elevated by the wind above the general level.

Way The movement of a boat through the water.

Way enough An order given, when rowing, to pull one more stroke only.

Ways Slipways, launching ways, timbers, over which a vessel may be moved.

Wear Change from one tack to the other, stern to wind. Gybe.

Weather Pass on the windward side of another boat or object. The area to windward is termed 'one's weather'.

Weather anchor The anchor lying to windward by which a ship rides when moored.

Weather a storm Survive it safely. Overcome a difficulty.

Weather helm A vessel which has a tendency to come up into the wind, and whose tiller has to be kept to windward to counteract it, is said to carry 'weather helm'.

Weather shore A shore which lies to windward of a vessel.

Weather side The side on which the wind blows.

Weatherbound Detained by foul winds.

Weed a line Remove loose stops and yarns left untidily on a line or stay.

Weeping Small quantities of water seeping through a boat's seams.

Weigh the anchor Raise and move the anchor from the bottom.

Weight the cable Lower a weight on a ring (or shackle) down a cable for a few fathoms, to assist riding in open waters.

Well The open space between deck erections. In fishing smacks the hold into which the fish are thrown. In yachts the cockpit. An exclamation signifying 'that will do'. Internal sounding compartments at the bottom of large vessels.

Well found Fully equipped.

Wending A method used to avoid making a hazardous gybe when running free, by luffing right round to the wind, going about, and paying off on the new tack.

West A cardinal point; the direction in which the sun sets.

Westing The distance made good to the westward.

Weston purchase A chain pulley constructed so that a load will remain suspended when no lift is being applied.

Wet dock A tidal basin or series of berths, as distinct from a floating or graving dock.

Whaler A vessel employed on whale fishing. A long narrow double-ended boat, which is extremely buoyant and stable.

Wharf A wooden or stone erection where ships may berth alongside for loading or unloading cargo.

Wheel The steering wheel; in large ships it is connected to the telemotor (see p 162), while in small boats it is fitted with a barrel around which the wheelropes (sometimes called the tiller ropes) are rove and/ or secured.

Wheelhouse, pilothouse An enclosed space sheltering the helmsman, the wheel, the steering compass, and the helm indicator.

Whelps Wooden brackets that may be affixed to a capstan barrel to enlarge its working diameter when hawsers are 'brought to'.

Where away? The request to a lookout that he should indicate the direction of an object reported.

Wherry A light shallow rowing boat used by watermen. The 'wherry' on the Norfolk Broads is a fast sailing barge.

Whip A lifting tackle which has one rope and a single block (see **Tackles**, p 163).

Whipping Binding the end of a line or rope to prevent the strands unlaying or fraying; the binding itself is termed a 'whipping'.

Whisker pole A jib stick (see p 97).

White ensign The ensign flown on the ensign staff by ships of the Royal Navy, and by members of the Royal Yacht Squadron when aboard their yachts.

White horses Waves whose tops are turned into breaking crests.

White rope Manila, cotton, and other rope which does not require tarring.

Winch A mechanical appliance used to obtain increased power by

bringing a hauling part to a revolving drum.

Wind A moving current of air, named according to the direction from which it blows and its force and speed.

Wind, wend a ship Turn a ship about, end for end.

Wind is heading Said when the wind changes to blow nearer the bows.

Wind shadow That area in which one sailing boat's wind may blanket another. Confused air therein is 'dirty wind'.

Windbound Unable to sail because of contrary winds.

Windflag A flag hoisted aloft to indicate wind direction.

Windjammer, windbag A fair-sized sailing ship.

Windlass A large barrel used for anchor work, or for hauling or hoisting by leading block. Small ones are revolved by crank handle, while in larger ships the term covers all forecastle machinery.

Windrode Riding head to wind at anchor, when the wind overcomes the tide.

Windsail

Windsail A wide-mouthed canvas shute, hoisted and guyed to the wind, to collect and divert air to compartments below.

Windscoop A metal scoop used in hot weather to collect and divert air through a porthole.

Windward Towards the wind.

Wing A side piece of a large awning. The long side of an upper deck. An overhanging platform extending to the ship's side

Wire rope Rope made of twisted iron or steel strands (see **Iron wire rope** and **Flexible steel wire rope**, pp 96 and 69).

Wiring A small-boat term for the stringers supporting the thwarts.

Wishbone ketch A ketch that has her mainsail area divided diagonally into two sails.

Wooden wings Leeboards (see p 105).

Work up the reckoning Determine the ship's position at any time by 'dead reckoning'.

Work with the tide Take advantage of a tide by keeping in midstream with the main flow, and, conversely, keep inshore away from the strongest flow when 'stemming the tide'.

Working A vessel is said to start working when her planking and timbers start straining so as to let water in.

Working load, strain See **Breaking strain**, p 28.

Working sails The essential mainsail and headsail.

Worm Fill the spaces or cant between the strands of a rope with yarns, to make a smooth surface for parcelling and serving.

Wreck A vessel that has been stranded, or badly injured, so as to be helpless. The ruins of a ship so destroyed. Flotsam and jetsam found on or near any coastline.

Wreck buoy A buoy, painted green, with the word 'wreck' on its side in white letters, positioned where a wreck is submerged. It may be can-shaped or conical, and should be passed on the mariner's port or starboard hand, accordingly.

Wreck-marking vessel A vessel positioned to mark a wreck; it is painted green, with the words 'wreck' in white on its sides; it also displays green balls or green lights to aid the mariner.

Wring a mast Bend, cripple, or strain a mast out of its natural position by bad setting and tautening of the shrouds.

Wung-out Goose-winged (see p 80).

Yacht A private pleasure vessel or boat, built specifically for racing or cruising, and with living accommodation for her crew.

Yacht Club An association formed by those interested in yachts and yachting, to promote the sport and regulate races, etc.

Yachting The navigation of a sailing, steam, or motor yacht.

Yacht-master's certificate A qualification obtained by passing an examination in coastal navigation, etc; it is open to all yachtsmen, and is an officially recognised standard.

Yachtsman One who owns or sails a yacht.

Yankee A popular design of jib topsail used in yacht racing.

Yard A spar hoisted and retained on a mast, for attaching and extending sails, hoisting flags, lights, etc.

Yard arm The extremity of a yard, outboard of the lifts.

Yarn Spun thread. A part of a strand of rope.

Yawing Not keeping a course. Swinging from side to side.

Yawl A two-masted vessel whose mainmast is tall and carries several sails but whose mizzen is short and carries a small sail over the stern to assist steering.

Yoke A fitting attached across the top of a rudder in a pulling boat, for use instead of a tiller.

Yoke lines Steering lines, held in the hand to control the yoke; in smart boats these are ornamental.

Yuloh An oar becketed to a thole pin, aft, for 'sculling' a boat.

Zephyr A soft gentle breeze; the west wind.

Zigzag sailing Sailing continuously on alternate tacks to make a mean course, eg when beating up a narrow channel.